TruthWorks

HELPING CHILDREN MAKE RIGHT CHOICES

BY AUTHOR

Josh McDowell

MANAGING WRITER

Dave Bellis

WRITERS

Cindy Ann Pitts   Christine Hockin Boyd   Bonnie Bruce
Mark Swadley

World Bridge Press
Nashville, Tennessee

World Bridge books are distributed to the trade
by Broadman and Holman Publishers
ISBN 0-8054-9827-3

Dewey Decimal Classification Number J231
Subject Heading: God–Will/Children–Religious Life

Printed in the United States
of America

World Bridge Press
127 Ninth Avenue, North
Nashville, Tennessee 37234

Contents

ACKNOWLEDGEMENT 4

INTRODUCTION 5

ADMINISTRATION 13

    Parents' Orientation Session 22

    Overhead Cell Masters 28

    Letter to Parents 34

    Truth Works Journal 35

    Parents' Handout 37

    Children's Daily Assignments 41

    Other *Right from Wrong* Resources 49

TRUTH WORKS SESSIONS

SESSION ONE ....Knowing Right from Wrong 53

SESSION TWO ....Honesty—*God Is True* 63

SESSION THREE ....Purity—*God Is Pure* 75

SESSION FOUR ....Love—*God Is Love* 86

SESSION FIVE ....Justice—*God Is Just* 97

SESSION SIX ....Mercy—*God Is Mercy* 105

SESSION SEVEN ....Respect—*God Is the Highest Authority* 114

SESSION EIGHT ....Self-Control—*God Is in Control* 122

Acknowledgment

I want to thank and humbly acknowledge a number of people who brought this project together. If not for their vision, dedication, and talent, this Leader's Guide and the activity books simply would not have been published. I want to acknowledge:

Jimmy Draper, Gene Mims, and Chuck Wilson with the Baptist Sunday School Board for their vision and commitment to the *Right from Wrong* message and campaign.

John Kramp for his skilled leadership, publishing vision for the *Right from Wrong* workbooks, and his untiring efforts as he championed this project on behalf of the publisher.

Dave Bellis, my associate of eighteen years, for directing every aspect of the *Right from Wrong* campaign and as managing writer of this project for developing and focusing the content and developing each product within the campaign into a coordinated campaign package.

Cindy Ann Pitts, Christine Hockin-Boyd, Bonnie Bruce, and Mark Swadley for their insights, writing skills, and passion for reaching children with the *Right from Wrong message*. They have labored hard and long to translate this message in a way that children can understand, which is no easy task. Special thanks, however, must be made to Cindy Pitts. Cindy molded and rewrote each lesson into a cohesive unit to bring about a focused and consistent presentation of the *Right from Wrong* message. Her insights, standard of excellence, and many years of experience with children are reflected in this project.

Larry Dry, Javier Elizondo, and Lynn Smith for their insights, educational design skills, persistence, and editing expertise as they input and structured each lesson and readied the manuscript for final publication.

Josh McDowell

Introduction

by Josh McDowell

You and I live in challenging times. Our newspapers report it: "Drugs Sold by Children," "Violence Erupts in Classroom," "Crime Takes Over Streets." News magazines document it. "The fraying of America's moral fabric has become a national obsession; 76 percent of Americans think we're in a spiritual and moral decline, according to a recent Newsweek poll." The Christian community fears it: "Based on a recent survey, the number one fear among Christian parents (pastors and youth leaders) is they will not be able to pass on their values to the next generation."

In our own 1994 national study conducted among churched youth ages 11-18, it showed that within a three month period:

    66 percent lied to a parent, teacher or another adult
    59 percent lied to one of their peers
    36 percent cheated on an exam
    23 percent intentionally tried to hurt someone

Additionally
    55 percent have engaged in sexual behavior by age 18
    50 percent say they are stressed out
    55 percent say they are confused

Something fundamentally wrong has happened in our culture that is shaking the very foundation of our society, especially our children. According to a recent news magazine, 68 percent of Americans are dissatisfied with the way things are going in this country and 80 percent of them believe our problem is the "moral decline of people in general." King David's question is as pertinent today as when he asked it: "When the foundations are being destroyed, what can the righteous do?" (Psalm 11:3).

The *Right from Wrong* campaign is designed to answer that question. That is why we are collaborating with over 40 denominational and para-church leaders **"to launch a nationwide grassroots effort to resource parents, grandparents, pastors, youth workers, children's workers, and Christian educators to equip youth and children to know right from wrong, enabling them to make right choices."**

OUR YOUTH ARE CONFUSED ABOUT TRUTH

As we examine our children's views about morality, it is apparent that the foundations upon which many parents, pastors, and youth leaders attempt to build are crumbling. Traditional biblical concepts are eroding; a Judeo-Christian world view is being undermined. Most of our youth lack the most basic moral perspectives that previous generations took for granted. Our study shows that an alarming 57 percent of our churched youth cannot state that an objective standard of truth even exists.

Only 15 percent of them disagree with the following statement: "What is right for one person in a given situation might not be right for another person who encounters the same situation." In other words, 85 percent of churched kids are liable to reason, "Just because it's wrong for you doesn't mean it's wrong for me." Their idea of the distinction between right and wrong is fluid, something that is subject to change, something that is relative and personal.

Forty-five percent of our churched youth could not disagree with the following statement, "Everything in life is negotiable." Almost half of our young people are unable or unwilling to recognize some things in life as nonnegotiable. It is unlikely, of course, that they realize the devastating effects of such a view, but that is part of the whole problem. Many of our youth are struggling with the concept of truth and how they are to apply it to their own lives and experiences. Our study indicates that our kids are confused about what truth is and who defines it; they are uncertain about what truths are absolute and what makes them absolute. If this is true of our teenagers, you can be certain our younger children are just as confused. Consequently, they are making conditional decisions, choosing what seems to be in their best interest at the time, without reference to any underlying principles to guide their behavior.

WHAT IS ABSOLUTE TRUTH?

Many of our young people simply do not understand or accept absolute truth–**that is, that which is true for all people, for all times, for all places**. Absolute truth is truth that is objective, universal, and constant.

We all have established various family rules and guidelines. For example, I have established a curfew with my 13-year-old daughter, specifying what time she should be home after a football game. I have told her, "It is not good to stay out beyond 11 p.m." I have set a firm guideline to be followed. If she obeys the curfew, she is right; if she violates it, she is wrong. I want my daughter to consider it a hard and fast rule. And, in most cases, she does.

But should we consider that guideline of being home by 11 p.m. after every football game an absolute truth? No. This guideline is not applicable to all people, at all times, in all places. Communities, states, and governments may create various ordinances, regulations, and laws that are to be obeyed, but they are not necessarily absolutes. Ordinances change, regulations expire, and some laws only apply in certain states. In fact, even the curfew rule for my daughter may change some day. An absolute truth, on the other hand, is objective, universal, and constant.

If our children are going to learn how to determine right from wrong, they must know what truths are absolute and why. They need to know what standards of behavior are **right for all people, for all times, for all places**. They need to know who determines truth and why.

WHY TRUTH MATTERS

You may say: "Come on, Josh, all this talk about absolutes seems so abstract. Do you really think that my children's views about truth will really make a difference in their behavior?" That is one of the astounding insights of this research. The study indicates that when our youth do not accept an objective standard of truth they become:

36 percent more likely to lie to a parent!

48 percent more likely to cheat on an exam!

2 times more likely to try to physically hurt someone!

2 times more likely to watch a pornographic film!

2 times more likely to steal!

3 times more likely to use illegal drugs!

6 times more likely to attempt suicide!

If your child fails to embrace truth as an objective standard that governs his life, the study shows it will make him:

65 percent more likely to mistrust people!
2 times more likely to be disappointed!
2 times more likely to be angry with life!
2 times more likely to be resentful!

How our youth think about truth has a definite affect on their behavior—the choices they make and the attitudes they adopt.

THERE IS HOPE

It is a frightening prospect to raise our children in the midst of a "perverse and crooked generation." There are no easy answers, but there is hope. It is not too late to reinforce the crumbling foundations. If you and I are willing to set aside the "quick fix" mentality and face the stark reality of what we as a Christian community have allowed (and perhaps unwittingly adopted ourselves), I believe there is hope.

First, I suggest you as the group leader obtain and read the book *Right from Wrong: What You Need to Know to Help Youth Make Right Choices*. As a truth apologetic it will provide you with a solid defense of truth. It is also the text this entire *Truth Works* program to children is based upon. Another resource I suggest your church utilize is the *Truth Matters for You and Tomorrow's Generation* five-part video series. There is also an eight-session *Truth Matters Workbook* for adults by the same title. There are other *Right from Wrong* workbooks that are directed to college students and junior high/high school students. There is also a video series to teenagers, as well as books and audio tapes. A listing of the *Right from Wrong* campaign resources are found on pages 47-50.

Meet with your pastor or church staff and discuss initiating a churchwide emphasis on *Right from Wrong*. Your church can begin this emphasis starting first with either the video series to adults and/or teenagers, or you can begin with the workbooks. The video series are highly motivational and challenges adults and teenagers, even nonbelievers, to embrace the concept of the right, moral choice process. The workbooks to adults, teenagers, and children, on the other hand, teaches them to apply the making-right-choices process to everyday life until it becomes a habit. The workbooks require a higher degree of spiritual interest and commitment in that they call for daily exercises to be completed between group sessions. Whatever combination of *Right from Wrong* resources you elect to use in a churchwide emphasis will enable you to powerfully reinforce and augment adults in their responsibilities to pass on biblical values to the next generation.

CHILDREN'S RESOURCES

The *Truth Works* activity books are directed to children in grades one through six in two different editions. The younger children's edition is for grades one through three, and the older children's edition is for grades four through six. The leader's guide provides instructions and activities for both workbooks.

This entire program is designed to help children determine right from wrong based upon God and His Word as the standard for making right moral choices. You will be teaching children a simple four-step process for making the right choices related to issues about honesty, purity, love, justice, mercy, respect, and self-control. The four steps are the Steps of Truth.

THE STEPS OF TRUTH

In each lesson we will be teaching children a four-step process to making right choices. The hope is that it will create a new way of thinking and acting as children learn how to make right choices based on God and His Word as their standard of right and wrong.

The following is a brief description of the process you will be teaching:

STEP 1: CONSIDER THE CHOICE

When faced with a moral choice, we want our children to first stop to consider what determines its rightness or wrongness.

Our culture has conditioned many to believe each individual has the right to determine what is right and wrong. Truth, in this view, is subjective and personal, and there is no absolute right and wrong that governs a person's life. In other words, it is up to the individual to determine the rightness and wrongness of her own attitudes or actions.

Ask:
What choices do I have and who determines what is right or wrong in this situation?

The Steps of Truth is a new way to process our moral choices. In this first step we must ask, "What choices do you have and who determines what is right or wrong in this situation?" This step erects a STOP sign of sorts to alert our children that their attitudes and actions are judged by someone other than themselves, and they are not to justify their behavior based on their own selfish interests.

STEP 2: COMPARE IT TO GOD

This next step answers the question, "Who determines what is right or wrong absolutely?" Here we want our children to ADMIT there is an absolute righteous God, and that they must compare their attitudes and actions to Him and His Word to determine whether they are right or wrong.

This step points them to the revelation of God in His written Word. His Word (Old and New Testament Scripture) gives all of us specific and absolute guidelines as to the rightness or wrongness of attitudes and actions. But these guidelines are not simply the "dos and don'ts" of the law, they are a reflection of the very nature and character of God Himself.

STEP 3: COMMIT TO GOD'S WAY

This third step is where the "rubber meets the road." This is decision time. Considering the choice and comparing it to God are necessary steps to show our children that their ways are not like God's ways. It shows all of us that our tendency is to justify, rationalize, and excuse ourselves, all in an attempt to legitimize our selfish interests and pleasures. When we compare our attitudes and actions to God as God, we ADMIT that His character and nature defines right and wrong absolutely. Those attitudes and actions that are like Him are considered right, and those attitudes and actions that are not like Him are considered wrong.

But when we commit to God's way, it means we turn from our selfishness and submit to God. We turn from those attitudes and actions that are unlike God and we SUBMIT to Him as Lord of our lives. We choose to rely on His power to live out His way in us.

Admit:

That God's character and nature defines right and wrong absolutely.

Submit:

To God as Lord of our lives and rely on His power to live out His way in us.

STEP 4: COUNT ON GOD'S LOVING MOTIVATION TO PROTECT AND PROVIDE

When we humbly ADMIT God's sovereignty and sincerely SUBMIT to His loving authority, we not only can begin to see clearly the distinctions between right and wrong, but we can also count on God's protection and provision. Here in this fourth step we want children to thank God for His loving protection and provision. This does not mean everything will be rosy. In fact, God says that we may suffer for righteousness sake. But such suffering has great rewards. Living according to God's way and allowing the Holy Spirit to live through us brings many spiritual blessings, like freedom from guilt, a clear conscience, the joy of sharing Christ, and most importantly the love and smile of God in our lives. Additionally, we enjoy many physical, emotional, psychological, and relational benefits when we are obedient to God. While God's protection and provision should not be our children's primary motivation to obey God, it provides a powerful reinforcement for them to choose the right and reject the wrong.

THE PURPOSE

The overall purpose of the *Truth Works* activity books is:

*   To teach children a model for making right moral choices through the Steps of Truth,

*   To teach children biblical truth about who God is,

*   To provide opportunity for children to practice making right choices, and

*   To provide children a safe place to discuss the choices they make.

Children need to know that God truly cares about the choices they make. "'For I know the plans I have for you,' declares the Lord, 'plans to prosper you and not to harm you, plans to give you hope and a future'" (Jeremiah 29:11). Ultimately, making right moral choices based upon God and His Word as our standard of right and wrong comes to trusting God. Do we really believe God has a plan to prosper us? If He does, and I assure you He does, then living in a relationship with Him is not only right, it is in our long-term best interest.

Thank God:
For His loving protection and provision.

This program will enable you to lead children to discover that a personal relationship with God is not only possible, but it is critical to them making right moral choices in life. You play a vital role in helping them understand that relationship. Together, with God's help, we can help children learn how to make right moral choices and help them discover a new and fresh relationship with God as well.

NOTE: The following administration section provides detailed instruction on how to conduct an effective children's program and the educational design of this program.

Administration

by Cindy Ann Pitts

INTRODUCTION

Truth Works is an eight-week program to teach children how to determine right from wrong, enabling them to make right choices. Combined with the other *Right from Wrong* resources, the entire church body can be equipped to reinforce the moral foundations of the family. Of course, you can use *Truth Works* independent from a churchwide *Right from Wrong* emphasis. Great times to use these materials with children can be for a Backyard Bible Club, Apartment Ministry Children's Bible Study, Children's Camp, or Sunday evening programming. Due to the large number of latchkey children in our society, many churches offer weekday, after-school care. That would also be an excellent time to offer this study for children. Several churches have week-night activities for adults. You could use this as an eight-week program for those times. Once you have decided how to use this program, you are ready for the next step.

SELECT LEADERSHIP

As with every program provided for children, you will need to enlist adults who can lead the program. As you seek leadership consider persons in your church who work with children regularly and effectively. School teachers, counselors, Sunday School teachers, and social workers in your church may be challenged by the opportunity to share their skills with children in this way.

There are three basic positions of leadership for this teaching plan. They are:

- **Truth Works Program Coordinator**—This person will oversee the entire program. You may be that person. For simplicity, this person will be referred to as program coordinator for the rest of this text.

- **Truth Works Study Group Leader**—This person will direct the work of one group of children. A group can consist of one child to a maximum of thirty children. This person is responsible for planning the hour session and leading the Truth Time and the Study Group Time. This person may also facilitate a small discussion group if you cannot secure enough leadership. This person will be referred to as study group leader.

- **Truth Works Discussion Group Leaders**—Each of these persons will lead a group of six to eight children in small group activities that relate to the Bible truths presented through the Truth Time and the Study Group Time. In the small discussion group the children will be challenged to apply the Steps of Truth, a process of making right choices, and discuss issues that affect their lives. This person will be referred to as discussion group leader.

The leaders you enlist should be growing Christians, members or active attendees of the church, able to sense that God is leading them to undertake this ministry, experienced workers with children, and persons around whom children enjoy being.

Prior to enlisting anyone for the responsibilities listed above, follow the procedures set by your church for enlisting members to work with children.

The responsibilities of the program coordinator are:
- To enlist the number of study group leaders and discussion group leaders needed for the program,

- To orient the leadership enlisted,

- To design publicity to encourage parents to enroll their children in this eight-week study,

- To register children and assign them to a group,

- To lead the Parent-Child Orientation Session,

- To purchase and distribute materials and supplies needed for the group,

- To calendar the dates for the sessions on the church calendar,

- To schedule rooms that will be used for the learning sessions, and

- To communicate with parents, study group leaders, and discussion group leaders.

The program coordinator may also serve as a study group leader and discussion group leader.

The responsibilities of the study group leader are:
- To plan each of the eight sessions for a group of children,

- To divide the children into small discussion groups of six to eight children,

- To lead the Truth Time activity, and

- To lead the Study Group Time.

The responsibilities of the discussion group leader are:
- To assist the study group leader with the Truth Time activity,

- To lead the Discussion Group Time, and

- To ead children in discussion as they work through the activities in *Truth Works*.

In addition, the Study Group Leader and Discussion Group Leader should be able to communicate effectively with children and keep things confidential, be good listeners, be committed to preparation, be committed to pray for the children in their groups, and be willing to read *Right from Wrong*.

DETERMINE THE GROUP STRUCTURE

To form your study groups, consider the number of children who register for the group and their ages. In larger programs study groups should be formed for every 24 to 30 children. In a smaller church you may have one study group.

The small discussion groups should be formed for every six to eight children. The ideal group size for children's discussion groups is six. Small groups allow for each child to actively participate.

For this teaching plan we suggest mixed groups of boys and girls. Best results are achieved when you can group the children closely by grade.

Encourage parents to make a commitment to help their children faithfully attend all eight sessions. It takes time for children in a discussion group to feel comfortable sharing with one another and with the adult discussion group leader. Each new personality will cause the group to readjust. It would be ideal if the same six children participated in the same discussion group all eight weeks.

However, *Truth Works* study groups are not a closed group program. A child may join the group at any time, and even if he only completes one session, he will have been taught the Steps of Truth choice making process. In session one the children will be introduced to the Steps of Truth. Each session thereafter they will learn a new truth and be led through the Steps of Truth. The more times a child is exposed to this making right choices model, the more ingrained this process will be in their minds and the more likely it will become a habit.

The sessions should last a minimum of one hour. If a group's dynamics are great and you feel they could use more time, feel free to work out that possibility with their parents. One and a half hours may be ideal for some older children. Encourage children to arrive on time and start promptly.

ASSIGN LEADERS TO EACH GROUP

Assign at least two adults to each group, a study group leader and discussion group leader. We suggest two adults because:

- Adult leaders can share responsibilities.

- Adult leaders can give each other honest feedback on the progress of the group.

- In the event of a problem, one adult can work on the problem while the other is free to keep leading the group. For example, if a child becomes sick or a discipline problem arises, one adult leader could give the child the time he needs.

ORDER RESOURCES

Order *Truth Works Leader's Guide* and activity books. There are three products you will need to order.

- *Truth Works: Helping Children Make Right Choices, Leader's Guide.* This is the leader's guide that you are reading right now! You will need one of these for each of your adult leaders. This guide has four sections. **Section One** describes the Children's Truth Works program. Helps are given to administer the program and orient volunteers to become effective group leaders. **Section Two** consists of the lesson plans for the parent orientation. The parent orientation is necessary if your church is not offering the *Right from Wrong* video series or the *Right from Wrong* workbooks for adults concurrently with the study for children. This orientation will help the parents know what their children are learning and how to reinforce the learning at home. **Section Three** contains the material that can be given out to the parents at the parents' orientation session. You are given permission to make copies of these parent handouts. You will distribute them during the parents' orientation. Even if your church is providing the adult *Right from Wrong* video and/or workbook programs, you may want to duplicate these handouts for the parents of the children enrolled in your groups. **Section Four** contains detailed instructions for leading the *Truth Works* sessions.

- *Truth Works: Younger Children's Edition.* You will need to have one of these for each younger child enrolled. This activity book is specifically designed for first through third graders.

- *Truth Works: Older Children's Edition.* This activity book is designed for fourth through sixth graders. You will need to purchase one for each older child you expect in your group.

These two children's activity books will be used during each session. The activities contained in them help to stimulate discussion. Each child's activity book should remain with the adult leaders until the end of session eight. The children may keep their activity books after the last session to remind them of the truths they have discussed and the choice making process they have learned.

To order your activity books and other *Right from Wrong* resources see pages 49-52 or visit your local Christian book store.

SCHEDULE THE SESSIONS

Set a time, date, and place for the *Truth Works* sessions. If your church is conducting a churchwide *Right from Wrong* emphasis, then your groups will meet concurrently with the adult, college, and youth groups. Otherwise, select any eight-week period in the life of your church that is good for consistent attendance.

If you conduct a parents' orientation, present the dates and times of the eight sessions. Ask the parents if they foresee any conflicts. If so, adjust the schedule to accommodate the majority of the children. A sample of a letter to be sent to parents is on page 34 for your consideration.

The best place for the *Truth Works* sessions will be rooms that are designated for children and have the appropriate child-sized furniture. During the study group time children will be seated in a semicircle around the study group leader. During the discussion group time children should be seated around tables since they will be using their activity books. They should be facing each other so that good discussion can take place.

PROMOTE THE TRUTH WORKS PROGRAM

Some ways to promote this program include:

- Articles in the church paper or newsletter

- A letter to the parents of all children on your roll and in your prospect file

- Announcements in the parents' Sunday School classes

- Direct calling of all parents whose children are enrolled in a church program or on the prospect file of your church

- Articles placed in the local papers

- Announcements made on local radio stations

CONDUCT
A LEADERS' ORIENTATION

As you recruit adults to assist you in teaching *Truth Works*, consider conducting an orientation meeting to discuss the entire program. Before the program begins, each leader accepting a position should read through all the sessions of the leader's guide and both children's editions. This will familiarize them with the materials they will be using and the supplies they will need. We also suggest each leader read *Right from Wrong*. Being acquainted with the content of the book and each session will help them prepare weekly for the upcoming sessions.

After each person has read *Right from Wrong* and the activity books, conduct your orientation meeting, discuss the program, and answer any questions your leaders might have. Make a list of the children you hope will attend the program and ask your leaders to pray daily for them and their families.

Emphasize the importance of this program in helping children learn to determine right from wrong. Remind them that they are assisting parents in their vital responsibility to pass on biblical values to the next generation.

To help your leaders be more effective, explain that you would like to discuss some important tips about being good and active listeners with the children.

BE A GOOD LISTENER

Become an active listener and a sensitive observer in order to evaluate just how much your instruction is being absorbed by your children.

Provide:
☐ *Use overhead cell master on page 28*

Children can communicate verbally by the words said or nonverbally through facial expression and body language. To be effective with children the adult teacher needs to be sensitive to what children are communicating, verbally and nonverbally.

Behavior or misbehavior can be a signal a child is sending. Through tears and facial twitches a child can express his emotional state. The sounds (sighs and groans) a child makes can indicate boredom, restlessness, disinterest, or even avoidance of participation.

Some good listening tips are:

- Provide good eye contact. When a child is speaking, look at the child.

- Ask your leaders to note how the other children react to the child who is speaking. It is better to have two leaders in the room because after the session the leaders can discuss impressions they had about the communication that was taking place.

- Lead the children to take turns speaking. Make discussion time as informal as possible.

- Take time to teach the children how to listen to each other. Encourage them to ask questions of each other and listen carefully.

- Summarize often what you have heard a child say or what the group has been saying.

- When you make a summary statement, give the children time to respond.

- Give a speaking child nonverbal clues of your undivided attention. Besides looking at the child, you can nod your head, make appropriate gestures, or lean toward her.

- Ask questions to guide them to the truth emphasized in the lesson.

- Communicate acceptance and honest concern. A child will not risk sharing if she feels that what she says will get her in trouble.

- Allow the children to feel free to express their emotions. Be sure a child that responds emotionally receives the affirmation he needs.

- Listen for recurring patterns. A child may be sending a message for help. Should you sense a recurring pattern, talk privately with the child after you dismiss the group.

- Do not feel that you have to solve all the children's problems. Many children suffer pain from troubled homes, and you are limited in what you can do. But you can teach them a process for making right moral choices in life regardless of their situations—choices that will result eventually in God's protection and provision for their lives.

CONDUCT A PARENT ORIENTATION SESSION

This session is designed to help parents understand the major concepts presented in *Right from Wrong* and to orient the parents to the making right choices process that will be taught to their children. This session is only necessary if the parents will not be going through the *Right from Wrong* workbook or video series for adults. You will find a step-by-step plan for conducting the Parents' Orientation Session on pages 22-27. A copy of the Parents' Handout to be distributed during the orientation is included on pages 37-40.

BATHE YOUR PREPARATION TIME IN PRAYER

The battle for the hearts and minds of our children and their families is not primarily an educational battle—it is a spiritual battle. When you teach the Steps of Truth, you are not simply addressing an educational issue, you are addressing a moral issue. Your children will come face-to-face with a choice of whether they will admit that God is the standard of right and wrong and whether they will submit to Him and commit to His ways.

Pray for your children and their families each day. Pray that they will see God in a new light, a God who lovingly wants to provide for them and protect them by enabling them to make right moral choices.

EVALUATE YOUR PROGRESS AND REMAIN FLEXIBLE

As you evaluate the progress of your groups, you may need to make changes. Prayerfully keep in mind what is in the best interest of the children. For example, if more children come to session one than you planned, praise the Lord! Then do all you can to provide more leadership and create more groups by session two.

Parents' Orientation Session

GUIDE TO AN EFFECTIVE PARENTS' ORIENTATION MEETING

NOTE: This meeting is necessary only if your church is not conducting the *Right from Wrong Truth Matters* video series or workbooks for adults concurrently with the *Truth Works* for children.

Session Goals

1. To inform parents about the eight-week *Truth Works* program for children

2. To introduce parents to the basic message of *Right from Wrong*

3. To acquaint parents with the Steps of Truth—the choice making process their children will be learning

4. To distribute the Parents' Handout and answer any questions parents may have about the *Truth Works* program

Leaders Need to Know

One leader may lead the parents' orientation meeting for all the *Truth Works* groups you have. The person who leads this meeting should have thoroughly read *Right from Wrong*, *Truth Works: Leader's Guide*, and both children's editions of the activity books.

This session can run concurrently with *Truth Works* session one.

PREPARING FOR THE SESSION

☐ Write the parents of the children enrolled in your children's program and invite them to the orientation meeting. (A sample letter is on page 34.)

☐ Obtain a supply of *Right from Wrong* books so that parents may purchase them at the close of the orientation.

☐ Obtain a copy of each of the *Truth Works* activity books.

☐ Select a room that will comfortably seat the number of people you expect. Provide name tags.

☐ Consider using an overhead projector for your presentation. See pages 28-33 for sample copies of overhead cells.

☐ Copy a sufficient quantity of the Parents' Handout found on pages 37-40 and the Children's Daily Assignments on pages 41-48.

LEADING THE SESSION

1. Greet parents at the door. Make name tags available.

2. Open in prayer.

3. Introduce the *Right from Wrong* campaign.
   According to a recent *Newsweek* poll, 76 percent of Americans think we are in spiritual and moral decline. Based on a recent survey, the number one fear among Christian parents is that they will not be able to pass their values to the next generation.

   Something fundamentally wrong has happened in our culture that is shaking the very foundation of our society, especially our children. Recent surveys also show that 68 percent of Americans are dissatisfied with the way things are going in this country and 80 percent of them believe our problem is the "moral decline of people in general." King David's question is as pertinent today as when he asked it, "When the foundations are being destroyed, what can the righteous do?" (Psalm 11:3).

   The *Truth Works* activity books help children know how to make right moral choices. By conducting this program we are attempting to supplement and augment your efforts to teach your children right from wrong.

It is not easy for young people to make right moral choices in today's society. Our culture has so conditioned them with self-centered views about the "rights" of the individual that it has affected their views of themselves and of God.

Consequently, many of them have a distorted perception of how to determine right from wrong. To reverse this trend we and our children need to learn a new way of thinking about truth and how it is determined. Therefore, Josh McDowell, speaker and author, along with 40 some denominations and para-church ministries are cooperating in a North American-wide campaign called *Right from Wrong*. I encourage you to obtain the book (hold up book). This book will give you insight into the problem and practical solutions in teaching your children right from wrong. These books are available for purchase at the close of this session.

Josh McDowell has collaborated with skilled children's writers and has created *Truth Works* for children (hold up activity books). This is the program we will be conducting with your children. We will be teaching them four simple steps to help them make right moral choices. These four steps are:

STEP 1: CONSIDER THE CHOICE

STEP 2: COMPARE IT TO GOD

STEP 3: COMMIT TO GOD'S WAY

STEP 4: COUNT ON GOD'S LOVING MOTIVATION
          TO PROTECT AND PROVIDE

Our plan is to incorporate these steps into real-life situations to help your children understand and embrace the truths about honesty, purity, love, justice, mercy, respect, and self-control. Allow me to walk through these four steps to acquaint you with how we plan to present these truths to your children.

4. Present the Four Steps.
STEP 1: CONSIDER THE CHOICE
When faced with a moral choice, we want our children to first stop to consider what determines its rightness or wrongness.

Our culture has conditioned many to believe each individual has the right to determine what is right and wrong. Truth, in this view, is subjective and personal and there is no absolute right and wrong that governs a person's life. In other words, it is up to the individual to determine the right-

---

Provide:
☐ *Copy of* **Right from Wrong**

Provide:
☐ *Copy of* **Truth Works** *activity books*

Provide:
☐ *Use overhead cell on page 29*
Ask:
What choices do you have and who determines what is right or wrong in this situation?

ness and wrongness of his own attitudes or actions.

The Steps of Truth is a new way to process our moral choices. In this first step we must ask, "What choices do you have and who determines what is right or wrong in this situation?" This step erects a STOP sign of sorts to alert our children that their attitudes and actions are judged by someone other than themselves, and they are not to justify their behavior based on their own selfish interests.

When we present your children with a moral question such as cheating, we will ask them to consider the choices they have available to them. They will be asked to list the benefits and the consequences of the different choices they have available to them. They will be asked to consider the choices and make the hand motions of arms outstretched, palms up, and hands moving up and down (demonstrate hand motion).

STEP 2: COMPARE IT TO GOD

This next step answers the question, "Who determines what is right or wrong absolutely?" Here we want the children to ADMIT there is an absolute righteous God and that they must compare their attitudes and actions to Him and His words to determine whether they are right or wrong.

This step points them to the revelation of God in His written Word. His Word (Old and New Testament Scripture) gives all of us specific and absolute guidelines as to the rightness or wrongness of attitudes and actions. But these guidelines are not simply the "dos and don'ts" of the law, they are a reflection of the very nature and character of God Himself.

The hand motion for Step 2 is like this. (Demonstrate the hand motion of folding your fingers together and pointing the index finger up like a steeple.)

STEP 3: COMMIT TO GOD'S WAY

This third step is where the "rubber meets the road"—this is decision time. Considering the choice and comparing it to God are necessary steps to show our children that their ways are not like God's ways. It shows all of us that our tendency is to justify, rationalize, and excuse ourselves, all in an attempt to legitimize our selfish interests and pleasures. When we compare our attitudes and actions to God as God, we ADMIT that His character and nature defines right and wrong absolutely. Those attitudes and actions that are like Him are considered right, and those attitudes and actions that are not like Him are considered wrong.

But when we commit to God's ways (demonstrate the hand motion of both thumbs up), it means we turn from our selfishness and submit to God. We turn from those attitudes and actions that are unlike God and SUBMIT to Him as Lord of our lives. We choose to rely on His power to live out His way in us.

Provide:

☐ *Use overhead cell on page 30*

Admit:

That God's character and nature defines right and wrong absolutely.

Provide:

☐ *Use overhead cell on page 31*

Submit:

To God as Lord of our lives and rely on His power to live out His way in us.

Thank God:

For His loving protection and provision.

STEP 4: COUNT ON GOD'S LOVING MOTIVATION
TO PROTECT AND PROVIDE

When we humbly ADMIT God's sovereignty and sincerely SUBMIT to His loving authority, we not only can begin to see clearly the distinctions between right and wrong, but we can also count on God's protection and provision. Here in this fourth step we want our children to thank God for His loving protection and provision (demonstrate the hand motions of arms arched over your head). This does not mean everything will be rosy. In fact, God says that we may suffer for righteousness sake. But such suffering has great rewards. Living according to God's way and allowing the Holy Spirit to live through us brings many spiritual blessings, like freedom from guilt, a clear conscience, the joy of sharing Christ, and most importantly the love and smile of God in our lives. Additionally, we enjoy many physical, emotional, psychological, and relational benefits when we are obedient to God. While God's protection and provision should not be our children's primary motivation to obey God, it certainly provides a powerful reinforcement for them to choose the right and reject the wrong.

5. Apply the Four Steps to honesty.

Now let me give you a practical example of how we will use these four steps. During a teaching time with your child we will set up a realistic scenario of a child who is tempted to take something that does not belong to him. For example: "Kelly and his friend were really thirsty, but they only had enough money for one can of soda. Kelly put his money in the soda machine. A can came out, and his money came back in the coin return. Consider the choice conflict. Kelly could use the money to buy his friend a can of soda. Or he could return the money to the people who owned the soda machine, but he and his friend would still be thirsty. How does Kelly decide what is right?"

We will then go through the hand motions of the Steps of Truth.

STEP 1: CONSIDER THE CHOICES
(demonstrate the hand motions)

We ask, "What are the choices that you have and who decides what's right and wrong in this situation?" *(God and His Word)*

STEP 2: COMPARE IT TO GOD
(demonstrate the hand motions)

In Exodus 20:15 and Leviticus 19:11-13, God says we are not to take things that do not belong to us.

Ask, "Why does God say that?" *(because God is true)* That is right. So to decide if it is right or wrong to keep the can of soda, we find out what God says.

STEP 3: COMMIT TO GOD'S WAYS
(demonstrate the hand motions)
Ask: "Because God is true, He wants us to be what?" *(honest)* "When we are honest, what will we not do?" *(steal)*

STEP 4: COUNT ON GOD'S LOVING MOTIVATION
TO PROTECT AND PROVIDE
(demonstrate the hand motions)
Ask, "When we make the right choices, what should we do?" *(thank God for protecting us and providing for us)*
Overall, our goal is to expose children to a new way of thinking and acting—a way to process the moral choices they encounter almost every day.

6. Distribute the Parents' Handout.
Next, distribute the *Truth Works* Parents' Handout. Briefly explain the handout the parents are receiving. The handout tells them what truths are taught to the children during each week and describes the Steps of Truth—process of making right choices.

Discuss the second handout, the Daily Assignments. In case a child misplaces his daily assignments, parents can still help him to complete the assignment. Assisting a child in his daily assignments will enable parents to take full advantage of the child's learning experience.

Distribute copies of *Truth Works*. Let the parents look through the activity books. Remind the parents that the activity books will stay with the leaders and will be used in the group sessions. Explain that after session eight the children can take their activity books home.

7. Review the schedule.
Look over with the parents the dates and times for the remaining seven sessions. Explain that your schedule accounts for holidays and other churchwide activities that may affect the regular group time.

8. Invite parents to ask questions and make comments.

9. Dismiss on time.

Provide:
☐ *Copies of Parents' Handout*
☐ *Copies of daily assignments*
☐ *Copies of* **Truth Works** *activity books*

Good Listening Tips

- Provide good eye contact.

- Observe how the other children react to the child who is speaking.

- Lead the children to take turns speaking.

- Take time to teach the children how to listen to each other.

- Summarize often.

- Give the children time to respond.

- Give a speaking child nonverbal clues of your undivided attention.

- Ask questions.

- Communicate acceptance and honest concern.

- Allow the children to feel free to express their emotions.

- Listen for recurring patterns.

- Do not feel that you have to solve all the children's problems.

Step 1
Consider
The Choice

Ask

What choices do I have and who
determines what is right or wrong in this situation?

Step 2
Compare It
To God

Admit

That God's character
and nature defines right and wrong absolutely.

Step 3
Commit
To God's Way

Submit

To God as Lord of our lives
and rely on His power to live out His way in us.

Step 4
Count On God's Loving Motivation To Protect and Provide

Thank God

For His loving motivation to protect and provide.

SAMPLE LETTER TO PARENTS TO INTRODUCE TRUTH WORKS

Dear (parents' names),

Raising children to love God and obey Him in today's world is not easy. We live in a day when young people, even young children, are thinking and doing things that were unthought of a generation ago. A recent survey reflected this when it showed the number one fear among Christian parents was that they would be unable to pass on their values to their children.

We here at the church want to help you in your responsibility to pass on biblical values to your children. We are joining in a nationwide effort called *Right from Wrong* launched by Josh McDowell. This campaign includes a program for children called *Truth Works* that we would like to conduct with your child from _____ to

_____.

We invite you to a Parents' Orientation Session this (date) at (location) from (time beginning and ending). During this orientation we will explain the *Right from Wrong* emphasis that we will be using to instruct your child and discuss how we can partner with you in your efforts to teach your child right from wrong.

If you have any questions, please do not hesitate to call me at (phone number). I hope to see you at the orientation meeting.

Sincerely,

(Your name and position)

My Truth Works Journal

Week 7

RESPECT: God Is the Highest Authority (1 Peter 2:17)

Because God is absolute Sovereign, we are to honor those in authority and show respect to others.

Choice I had this week

_____

Choice I made

_____

Did I please God?

_____

Week 8

SELF-CONTROL: God Is in Control (1 Peter 5:8)

Because God is in control, we are to yield to Him and maintain self-control.

Choice I had this week

_____

Choice I made

_____

Did I please God?

_____

Week 1
MAKING RIGHT CHOICES

Through the Steps of Truth (Deuteronomy 6:18)

Choice I had this week

_____

Choice I made

_____

Did I please God?

_____

Week 2
HONESTY: God Is True (Leviticus 19:11-13)

Because God is true, we are to live honestly before others.

Choice I had this week

_____

Choice I made

_____

Did I please God?

_____

Week 3
PURITY: God Is Pure (1 Corinthians 6:20)

Because God is pure, we are to keep our thoughts, words, and deeds pure and right.

Choice I had this week

_____

Choice I made

_____

Did I please God?

_____

Week 4
LOVE: God Is Love (Matthew 22:37-39)

Because God is love, we are to treat others as we are to treat ourselves

Choice I had this week

_____

Choice I made

_____

Did I please God?

_____

Week 5
JUSTICE: God Is Just (Deuteronomy 32:40)

Because God is just, we are to treat others fairly.

Choice I had this week

_____

Choice I made

_____

Did I please God?

_____

Week 6
MERCY: God Is Mercy (Zechariah 9:7)

Because God is mercy, we are to forgive others of their offenses against us.

Choice I had this week

_____

Choice I made

_____

Did I please God?

_____

TRUTH WORKS
PARENTS' HANDOUT

Truth Works activity book is a moral reinforcement program of the church to assist you in your goals to instill biblical values in your children. During eight sessions your child will be taught:

WEEK 1 _____
Making Right Choices through the Steps of Truth
(Deuteronomy 6:18)

This week children learned the four basic steps to follow in choosing to do what is right (the 4c's or the Four Steps of Truth).

STEP 1: CONSIDER THE CHOICE
ASK: "What choices do I have and who determines what is right or wrong in this situation?"

STEP 2: COMPARE IT TO GOD
ADMIT God is God and compare our attitudes and actions to His Word which reflects His character and nature.

STEP 3: COMMIT TO GOD'S WAY
Turn from our selfish ways and **SUBMIT** to God's sovereign lordship.

STEP 4: COUNT ON GOD'S LOVING MOTIVATION
TO PROTECT AND PROVIDE
THANK GOD for the protection and provision He gives us when we do what is right.

One of the exercises they did helps them see that if they want to do what is right, they have to have a healthy fear of God. There are four reasons why we fear God:

(1) He is God (Psalm 46:10).

(2) He is the giver of all things (James 1:17).

(3) He is the judge of good and evil (Ecclesiastes 12:14).

(4) It is for our own good (Jeremiah 32:39).

Look for opportunities this week to talk to your child about the fear of God. Help your child understand that in moral issues, God is the One that makes the final judgment.

WEEK 2 _____
Honesty—God Is True (Leviticus 19:11-13)
Because God is true, we are to live honestly before others.

This week children learned about not lying, cheating, or stealing. You will find below two of the case studies the children discussed. Talk to your child about immediate gratification and long-term benefits of making a right choice or a wrong choice in the situation described in the given case study.

> *Case Study for Younger Children:* You go to use the pay phone at your school. When you deposit your quarter, several quarters come out the return slot. You take all the quarters and return them to the principal's office.

> *Case Study for Older Children:* You ask your parents if you can go to the library for two hours. You go to the library for an hour and forty-five minutes and the video arcade for fifteen minutes. When your parents ask how the library trip was, you say, "Fine. I checked out two new books."

WEEK 3 _____
Purity—God Is Pure (1 Corinthians 6:20)
*Because God is pure, we are to keep our thoughts, words,
and deeds pure and right.*

This week children learned about keeping their bodies and minds clean. In one of the exercises the children were asked to think of one time when they were pressured by others not to keep their minds or bodies clean. Look for an opportunity this week where you and your child together apply the Steps of Truth to a situation you, your child, or a third person is facing where you will be tempted to not keep your mind or body clean. Possible topics for discussion are: TV shows and movies we watch and whether they help us keep our minds and bodies clean and pure; use of drugs (for older children).

The children's materials do not deal specifically with the subject of sex. Instead, the discussion is framed in terms of how God wants us to keep our minds and bodies clean and pure. We talked about not reading books, magazines, or watching TV programs that use bad language and show things God commands us not to do.

WEEK 4 _____
Love—God Is Love (Matthew 22:37-39)

Because God is love, we are to treat others as we are to treat ourselves.

This week children learned about loving others. Children were asked to think of a situation when they found it hard to love someone. Then they applied the Steps of Truth to that specific situation. Talk to your child about some things he could do to show love to a person he finds hard to love. Help your child choose an appropriate action he could take. Ask your child to tell you when he has done it and compliment him.

WEEK 5 _____
Justice—God Is Just (Deuteronomy 32:4)

Because God is just, we are to treat others fairly.

In this session children learned about how we feel and act when life is unfair. The children used the following case study to discuss the issue of justice. Use the case study to talk with your child about whether she thought Sara had done the right thing.

> *Case Study:* Sara was selling candy bars for her class during recess. Renee wanted to buy one. Renee had been mean to Sara and had thrown her notebook paper in the mud. Although the candy bars were only twenty-five cents, Sara sold Renee a candy bar for forty cents. Renee paid it because she did not realize it was only twenty-five cents. Sara kept the extra fifteen cents to help pay for the notebook paper Renee had ruined.
> Jury: Was Sara right in what she did?

WEEK 6 _____
Mercy—God Is Mercy (Zechariah 9:7)

Because God is mercy, we are to care for people in need, and we are to forgive others when they offend us.

This week children learned about mercy. We show mercy when we forgive those who hurt us and when we care for those in need. Ask your child about the case study below and what he would have chosen to do in that situation.

> *Case Study:* Your friend is sick. You want to buy a present for him. All your allowance is gone. You have been saving to buy a new video game. If you spend money for a present, you will not have enough to buy the video game. What will you do?

WEEK 7 _____
Respect—God Is the Highest Authority (1 Peter 2:17)
Because God is absolute Sovereign, we are to honor those in authority and show respect to others.

This week children learned about respect. They learned about the protections and provisions we can count on when we respect others. Play a game where you and your child are going to mark on a card every time you are together and you see someone showing respect. Whoever notices first the instance of showing respect is responsible for letting the other one know what is taking place. Talk to your child about the provisions and protections of showing respect as you watch those around you showing respect.

WEEK 8 _____
Self-Control—God Is in Control (1 Peter 5:8)
Because God is in control, we are to yield to Him and maintain self-control.

This week children learned about why it is right to restrain their wants and appetites and why it is wrong to demand to get what they want and when they want it.

Talk to your child about one area where both of you are going to practice exercising self-control this week. Check with one another on Wednesday to see how well you have done. Then check again at the end of the week. Look for opportunities to compliment your child when he exercises self-control in any area.

Instructors teaching this program to your children are:

Honesty
God Is True

Ask a parent or other adult to read with you the activities for each day. Answer the questions. Fill in the blanks with the words from this list (some words are used more than once): perfect, wrong, Father, true, work, truth, steal, laws, right. (Use the *New International Version* of the Bible.)

MONDAY
What it means to be honest
Memory Verse: Leviticus 19:11-13

Do not steal. Do not lie. Do not deceive one another. Do not swear falsely . . . Do not defraud your neighbor or rob him.
Do: When you have memorized the verse above, write it on the back of this page or say it from memory to an adult.
Pray: "Dear God, help me to be honest all the time."

TUESDAY
God is true.
We should be true
Read: John 14:6

Do: Jesus is God. What is Jesus like? "Jesus answered, 'I am the way and the _____ and the life. No one comes to the _____ except through me.'"
Pray: "Dear God, help me to be true like Jesus is true."

WEDNESDAY
God does not lie.
We should not lie
Read: Psalm 119:160

Do: Is God's Word true? "All your words are _____; all your righteous _____ are eternal."
Pray: "Dear God, help me to tell the truth, even when it is difficult."

THURSDAY
God does not cheat.
We should not cheat
Read: Deuteronomy 32:4

Do: Is God fair? "He is the Rock, his works are _____, and all his ways are just. A faithful God who does no _____, upright and just is he."
Pray: "Dear God, keep me from being tempted to cheat, and when I am tempted, help me do what is right."

FRIDAY
God does not steal.
We should not steal
Read: Ephesians 4:28a

Do: What does God's Word say to those who steal? "He who has been stealing must _____ no longer, but must _____, doing something useful with his own hands."
Pray: "Dear God, help me not to steal. Help me do what is right."

Knowing
Right from Wrong

Ask a parent or other adult to read with you the activities for each day. Answer the questions. Unscramble the words to check your answers. (Use the *New International Version* Bible.)

MONDAY
Fearing God
Memory Verse: Deuteronomy 6:18

Do: Find the memory verse in your Bible and memorize it. When you have memorized it, write it below or say it from memory to an adult. _____
Pray: "Dear God, help me to do what is right and good."

TUESDAY
Consider the choice
Read: Exodus 23:2

Do: What do you do when your friends want you to do something wrong? "Do not follow the c_____ d *(orw)* in doing wrong."
Pray: "Dear God, help me not to follow my friends when they make bad choices."

WEDNESDAY
Compare it to God
Read: Job 34:12

Do: What is God like? Does He ever do anything wrong? "It is unthinkable that God would do w_____ g *(orn)*."
Pray: "Dear God, I want to be like You. Help me make my choices based on what You are like."

THURSDAY
Commit to God's way
Read: Proverbs 3:5

Do: How do I choose to follow God's way? "T_____ t *(usr)* in the Lord with all your heart and lean not on your own understanding."
Pray: "Dear God, help me to trust You and choose Your right way."

FRIDAY
Count on God's protection and provision
Read: Psalm 18:2

Do: Unscramble the words that describe God's protection/provision: "The Lord is my r_____ k *(co)*, my fortress and my deliverer; my God is my rock, in whom I take refuge. He is my sh_____ d *(lie)* and the horn of my salvation, my stronghold."
Pray: "Thank You, God, for protecting me and providing for me."

Challenge Activities

1. God is honest. We should be honest.

Read: Isaiah 45:19b

Do: When God speaks, what does He speak?
"I, the Lord, speak the _____; I declare what is _____."

Pray: "Dear God, let me speak true and honest words."

2. Write about when a friend was dishonest to you (he lied to you, cheated you, or stole from you).

_____

_____

How did his dishonesty make you feel? _____

What did it do to your friendship? _____

How can you show forgiveness to this friend? _____

_____

God is also hurt when we are dishonest, but He will forgive us whenever we confess our sin to Him.

Read 1 John 1:9.

What is God faithful to do? _____

Live a life of truth and honesty. When you are dishonest, ask God to forgive you and keep trying to live honestly.

Challenge Activities

1. Read: Proverbs 1:7

The fear of the Lord is the beginning of knowledge.

When we talk about fearing God, what are we talking about? Choose the right answers from the list and write them in the space below:

forgetting Him	respecting Him
looking up to Him	listening to Him
honoring Him	being mean to Him
ignoring Him	obeying Him
wanting to please Him	

_____

_____

_____

_____

2. Draw the four hand motions for the Steps of Truth.

1. CONSIDER THE CHOICE

2. COMPARE IT TO GOD

3. COMMIT TO GOD'S WAY

4. COUNT ON GOD'S CARE

3. Write about one of the choices you had to make this week where you used the Steps of Truth (use your journal). Talk to a parent or other adult about it.

Love
God Is Love

Ask a parent or other adult to read with you the activities for each day. (Use the *New International Version* of the Bible when looking up a Bible verse.)

MONDAY
Show God you love Him
Memory Verse: Matthew 22:37-39

Do: Take time to learn the verse and say it from memory to an adult.
Think of two ways you show God you love Him. Write them here and then do them.

1. _____
2. _____

Pray: "Dear God, help me to show You every day how much I love You."

TUESDAY
Show love to your family
Read: 1 John 4:7

Do: Make a list of the people who live with you.

_____
_____
_____

How can you obey this verse today by loving the people with whom you live?

Do the ideas that come to your mind.
Pray: "Dear God, help me to show my love to my family."

WEDNESDAY
Show love to others
Read: 1 John 3:11
This verse is almost the same as the one we read yesterday.

Do: Think of someone with whom you do not live for whom you can do something kind. Ask your parents to help you do something kind for him or her.
Pray: "Dear God, help me to show my love for _____ this week."

THURSDAY
Love those who are mean to you
Read: Matthew 5:44

Do: This is a hard verse! Can you think of someone who is hard for you to love? Maybe a bully at school? Think of something nice you can do for him or her. Try to do it soon.
Pray: "Dear God, help me to love _____. She/he is hard to love, and I need your help to be able to love her/him."

Purity
God Is Pure

Ask a parent or other adult to read with you the activities for each day. (Use the *New International Version* of the Bible when looking up a Bible verse.)

MONDAY
Choose to honor God
Memory Verse: 1 Corinthians 6:19-20

Do you not know that your body is a temple of the Holy Spirit, who is in you, whom you have received from God? You are not your own; you were bought at a price. Therefore honor God with your body.

Do: Highlight or underline the last five words of this verse. Take time to learn the verse and say it from memory to an adult. How can you choose to honor God with your body today?

_____

Pray: Ask God to help you honor Him in everything you do today.

TUESDAY
Choose to please God when you watch TV
Read: Look at the words you marked yesterday in 1 Corinthians 6:20

Do: How many hours of TV do you watch in one day? _____ Before you watch TV today, pray and ask God to help you know when something is said or done on the show that does not please Him. Decide to quit watching the shows that are not good for you.
Pray: Ask God to help you watch only those TV shows that do not cause you to have impure thoughts.

WEDNESDAY
Choose to use words that please God
Read: 1 Timothy 5:22.

Do: Write the last three words of the verse here _____. Are there any words that you need to quit using? Decide to use words today that please God.
Pray: Ask God to help you use words that are pure.

THURSDAY
Choose to honor God with your body
Read: Review 1 Corinthians 6:20 (the last five words).

Do: Draw a picture of one thing you can do to take good care of your body. Put the picture in a place that will remind you to honor God today.
Pray: Ask God to help you honor Him by taking good care of your body.

Challenge Activities

FRIDAY

God loved you first

Read: 1 John 4:19

Do: Circle the answer to the question: Who loved first, God or us?

Pray: Thank God for loving you. Sing a song to Him.

1. Do: Think of the most important thing you learned this week. Write it down below. _____

2. Think of one Bible story that talks about God loving us. Draw a picture from that Bible story.

3. Write about one of the choices you had to make this week where you had a chance to show love to someone (use your journal). Talk to a parent or other adult about it.

Challenge Activities

FRIDAY

Choose to be pure like God is pure

Read: 1 John 3:3

Do: Find the Bible verse in your Bible and fill in the blanks below.

Everyone who has this _____ in him _____ him- self, just as he is _____.

Pray: Ask God to help you be pure like He is pure.

1. What does pure mean? Circle the words that describe what pure means.

dirty	good	clean	spotless
bad	evil	clear	perfect

2. Write a prayer to God, thanking Him for the things you can do with your body that are pleasing to Him. _____

3. Write about one of the choices you had to make this week where you had a chance to be pure (use your journal). Talk to a parent or other adult about it.

Mercy
God Is Mercy

Ask a parent or other adult to read with you the activities for each day.
(Use the *New International Version* of the Bible when looking up a Bible verse.)

MONDAY
God wants you to show compassion to others
Memory Verse:
Zechariah 7:9

This is what the Lord Almighty says, *"Administer true justice . . . Show mercy and compassion to one another."*
Do: When you have memorized the verse above, turn the page and write it on the back of this page or say it from memory to an adult.
Pray: Ask God to help you grow up to be a person who shows compassion to others.

TUESDAY
Show compassion for the sick
Read:
Matthew 25:36

Do: Think of someone who is sick. Make a card. Mail or take it to the person. Taking the time to make something shows you care. By doing this, you are showing mercy.
Pray: Ask God to help the person who is sick and the family. Pray also for the doctors who are taking care of the sick person.

WEDNESDAY
Show compassion for the poor
Read:
Leviticus 19:10

Do: Give part of your allowance to help feed the hungry. Ask a parent or an adult to help you choose where to give your money.
Pray: Ask God to bless what you have given to feed the poor. Ask Him to multiply what you have given.

THURSDAY
Show compassion for someone who has treated you unkindly
Read: Mark 11:25

Do: Think of someone who has treated you unkindly. Tell God that you are willing to forgive the person. Then forget what he did to you. This is the way to show that you truly forgive.
Pray: Ask God to help you forgive that person. Ask God to help you treat that person as if he had never been unkind to you.

FRIDAY
Show compassion to those that are unhappy
Read:
1 Corinthians 16:18

Do: Think of someone who is unhappy. Draw a happy picture and take or mail it to that person. This is a way to show you care. When you care enough to do something, you are showing mercy.
Pray: Ask God to help you refresh the spirit of the person who is unhappy.

Justice
God Is Just

Ask a parent or other adult to read with you the activities for each day.
(Use the *New International Version* of the Bible when looking up a Bible verse.)

MONDAY
God is just so I should be just
Memory Verse:
Deuteronomy 32:4

He is the Rock, his works are perfect, and all his ways are just. A faithful God who does no wrong, upright and just is he.
Do: When you have memorized the verse above, turn the page and write it on the back of this page or say it from memory to an adult.
Pray: "Dear God, help me to be just when I play and when I work."

TUESDAY
God takes care of those who are just
Read:
2 Thessalonians 1:6

Do: God is what? _____.
Think of someone you have treated unfairly. Use the Steps of Truth to decide how to treat her the next time.
Pray: "Dear God, help me to be fair with others even when they are not being fair with me."

WEDNESDAY
God wants to be good to us
Read: Isaiah 30:18

Do: What does God want to do? He wants to show us
_____.
Pray: "Dear God, thank You for showing us mercy and for being just."

THURSDAY
God loves justice
Read: Psalm 99:4

The King [God] is mighty, he loves justice—you have established equity . . . you have done what is just and right.
Do: Talk to a parent or other adult about why God would love justice (answer on the back of the page).
Pray: "Dear God, thank You for not having favorites. Help me to be the same way with the people around me."

KEY WORDS

*Mighty.....*very powerful

*Justice.....*to do what is right and fair

*Equity.....*to treat others without having favorites

Challenge Activities

1. Read Luke 6:35. Think of one person whom you really have a hard time forgiving. Pray for that person every day for five days. Ask God to bless this person and to help you forgive him.

☑ *Check the box after you have prayed each time.*

☐ Day 1

☐ Day 2

☐ Day 3

☐ Day 4

☐ Day 5

2. Write about one of the choices you had to make this week where you had a chance to show mercy to someone (use your journal). Talk to a parent or other adult about it.

Do: Whose example should you follow? Name one way you can do what the Bible says.

Read: _____

Deuteronomy 16:20

Pray: "Dear God, help me to do what is just and right even when no one but You is watching."

Challenge Activities

1. *Read:* Deuteronomy 32:4

Do: Admit that God is just. Admit that you should be just, too. God's ways are _____ what?

Pray: "Dear God, help me to be just like You—not to have any favorites, to treat everyone right, and to love to do what is right all the time, everywhere."

2. Write about one of the choices you had to make this week where you had a chance to be fair and just to someone (use your journal). Talk to a parent or other adult about it.

[Answer to Thursday's question: God loves justice because He wants for us to get along and live in peace. When we treat one another justly, we can live in peace and get along with each other better.]

Self-Control
God Is in Control

Ask a parent or other adult to read with you the activities for each day. (Use the New International Version of the Bible when looking up a Bible verse.)

MONDAY
God wants to help you have self-control
Memory Verse:
1 Peter 5:8

Be self-controlled and alert.
Do: When you have memorized the verse above, turn the page and write it on the back of this page or say it from memory to an adult.
Pray: Ask God to help you be alert to the things that might tempt you to lose control.

TUESDAY
God shows self-control
Read: Genesis 6:5-22; 7:1-8:17; 9:13-15

Do: Read this Bible story together with a parent. Discuss how God showed self-control. What was the beautiful promise that God gave us as a reminder each time we see it in the sky? ___ a i ___ b ___ w
Pray: Thank God for showing self-control in dealing with us.

WEDNESDAY
Show self-control when we speak
Read: Ephesians 5:4

Do: Write below the three things the verse says we should not do when we talk.
1.
2.
3.
Write the one thing the verse says we should do when we talk. ___
Pray: Ask God to help you show self-control when you talk to your parents, your teachers, your friends, and others.

THURSDAY
Show self-control when you feel angry
Read: Colossians 3:8

Do: Write below two things the verse mentions where you can show self-control.
1.
2.
Pray: Ask God to help you show self-control when you get angry.

Respect
God Is the Highest Authority

Ask a parent or other adult to read with you the activities for each day. (Use the *New International Version* of the Bible when looking up a Bible verse.)

MONDAY
God wants us to show respect to others
Memory Verse:
1 Peter 2:17

Show proper respect to everyone: Love the brotherhood of believers, fear God, honor the king.
Do: When you have memorized the verse above, turn the page and write it on the back of this page or say it from memory to an adult.
Pray: Thank God for the people around you to whom you are always happy to show respect.

TUESDAY
Show respect to God
Read: Exodus 3:4-6

Do: Whom did God ask to remove his sandals? ___
Was this showing respect to God? ___
Pray: Ask God for a good attitude when talking to Him.

WEDNESDAY
Show respect for leaders
Read: 1 Samuel 24:8-10

Do: What did David do to show respect for King Saul?
___
___
Pray: Ask God to help you show respect for leaders.

THURSDAY
Show respect for those no one wants to respect
Read:
1 Samuel 30:11-15

Do: What group of people left a slave to die? ___
David and his men fed the slave a cake of pressed f___g___ and two cakes of ra___s___n___.
Pray: Tell God that you will treat with respect the people others do not want to respect.

FRIDAY
Show respect for your parents
Read: Exodus 20:12

Honor your father and your mother, so that you may live long in the land your God has given you.
Do: In the Bible verse above, circle the word that tells you what you are supposed to do. You honor your parents when you show respect for them and obey them.
In the Bible verse above, underline the promise that God gives you if you obey the command.
Pray: Ask God to help you show respect to your parents every day and everywhere.

FRIDAY

Prepare yourself to show self-control

Do: Talk to a parent or other adult about how we can be prepared to act right when an opportunity comes to show self-control.

Read: 1 Peter 1:13

Pray: Pray and ask God to help you be self-controlled in all your actions.

Challenge Activities

1. Write about one of the choices you had to make this week where you had a chance to show self-control (use your journal). Talk to a parent or other adult about it.

2. Write one time when it is very hard for you to show self-control. _____

   Choose to pray every day for five days and ask God to help you show self-control with this one thing. Ask one of your parents or an adult to help you pray about this.

   ☑ *Check the box for every day you remember to pray.*

   ☐ Day 1

   ☐ Day 2

   ☐ Day 3

   ☐ Day 4

   ☐ Day 5

Challenge Activities

1. Draw a picture of one time this week when you saw someone showing respect. Talk to a parent or other adult about it

2. Write about one of the choices you had to make this week where you had a chance to show respect to someone (use your journal). Talk to a parent or other adult about it.

Passing on the Truth to Our Next Generation

The "Right From Wrong" message, available in numerous formats, provides a blueprint for countering the culture and rebuilding the crumbling foundations of our families.

Read It and Embrace a New Way of Thinking

The Right From Wrong Book to Adults

Right From Wrong - What You Need to Know to Help Youth Make Right Choices
by Josh McDowell & Bob Hostetler

Our youth no longer live in a culture that teaches an objective standard of right and wrong. Truth has become a matter of taste. Morality has been replaced by individual preference. And today's youth have been affected. Fifty-seven percent (57%) of our churched youth cannot state that an objective standard of right and wrong even exists!

As the centerpiece of the "Right From Wrong" Campaign, this life-changing book provides you with a biblical, yet practical, blueprint for passing on core Christian values to the next generation.

Right From Wrong, Trade Paper Book
ISBN 0-8499-3604-7

The Truth Slayers Book to Youth

The Truth Slayers - The Battle of Right From Wrong
by Josh McDowell & Bob Hostetler

This book—directed to youth—is written in the popular NovelPlus format and combines the fascinating story of Brittney Marsh, Philip Milford and Jason Withers and the consequences of their wrong choices with Josh McDowell's insights for young adults in sections called "The Inside Story."

The Truth Slayers conveys the critical "Right From Wrong" message that challenges you to rely on God's word as the absolute standard of truth in making right choices.

The Truth Slayers, Trade Paper Book
ISBN 0-8499-3662-4

Hear It and Adopt a New Way of Teaching

Right From Wrong Audio for Adults
by Josh McDowell

What is truth? In three powerful and persuasive talks based on the book *Right From Wrong*, Josh McDowell provides you, your family, and the church with a sound, thorough, biblical, and workable method to clearly understand and defend the truth. Josh explains how to identify absolutes and shows you how to teach youth to determine what is absolutely right from wrong.

Right From Wrong, Audio–104 min.
ISBN 0-8499-6195-5

See It and Commit to a New Way of Living

Video Series to Adults

Truth Matters for You and Tomorrow's Generation
Five-part Video Series featuring Josh McDowell

Josh McDowell is at his best in this hard-hitting series that goes beyond surface answers and quick fixes to tackle the real crisis of truth. You will discover the reason for this crisis, and more importantly, how to get you and your family back on track. This series is directed to the entire adult community and is excellent for building momentum in your church to address the loss of values within the family.

This series includes five video sessions, a comprehensive Leader's Guide including samplers from the five "Right From Wrong" Workbooks, the *Right From Wrong* book, the *Truth Slayers* book, and a 12-minute promotional video tape to motivate adults to go through the series.

Truth Matters, Adult Video Series
ISBN 0-8499-8587-0

Video Series to Youth

Setting You Free to Make Right Choices
Five-part Video Series featuring Josh McDowell

Through captivating video illustrations, dynamic teaching sessions, and creative group interaction, this series presents students with convincing evidence that right moral choices must be based on a standard outside of themselves. This powerful course equips your students with the understanding of what is right from what is wrong.

The series includes five video sessions, Leader's Guide with reproducible handout including samplers from the five "Right From Wrong" Workbooks, and the *Truth Slayers* book.

*Setting You Free to Make
Right Choices*, Youth Video Series
ISBN 0-8499-8585-4

Practice It and Make Living the Truth a Habit

Workbook for Adults

Truth Matters for You and Tomorrow's Generation
Workbook by Josh McDowell with Leader's Guide

The "Truth Matters" Workbook includes 35 daily activities that help you to instill within your children and youth such biblical values as honesty, love, and sexual purity. By taking just 25 - 30 minutes each day, you will discover a fresh and effective way to teach your family how to make right choices–even in tough situations.

The "Truth Matters" Workbook is designed to be used in eight adult group sessions that encourage interaction and support building. The five daily activities between each group meeting will help you and your family make right choices a habit.

Truth Matters, Member's Workbook ISBN 0-8054-9834-6
Truth Matters, Leader's Guide ISBN 0-8054-9833-8

Workbook for College Students

Out of the Moral Maze
by Josh McDowell with Leader's Instructions

Students entering college face a culture that has lost its belief in absolutes. In today's society, truth is a matter of taste; morality of individual preference. "Out of the Moral Maze" will provide any truth-seeking collegiate with a sound moral guidance system based on God and His Word as the determining factor for making right moral choices.

Out of the Moral Maze, Member's Workbook with
Leader's Instructions
ISBN 0-8054-9832-X

Workbook for Junior High and High School Students
Setting You Free to Make Right Choices
by Josh McDowell with Leader's Guide

With a Bible-based emphasis, this Workbook creatively and systematically teaches your students how to determine right from wrong in their everyday lives–specifically applying the decision-making process to moral questions about lying, cheating, getting even, and premarital sex.

Through eight youth group meetings followed each week with five daily exercises of 20-25 minutes per day, your teenagers will be challenged to develop a life-long habit of making right moral choices.

Setting You Free to Make Right Choices, Member's Workbook
ISBN 0-8054-9828-1
Setting You Free to Make Right Choices, Leader's Guide
ISBN 0-8054-9829-X

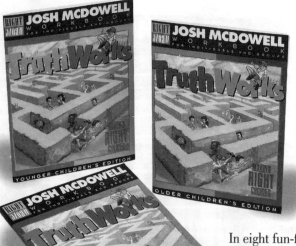

Workbook for Children
Truth Works - Making Right Choices
by Josh McDowell with Leader's Guide

To pass on the truth and reclaim a generation, we must teach God's truth when our children's minds and hearts are young and pliable. Creatively developed, "Truth Works" is two workbooks, one directed to younger children grades 1 - 3 and one to older children grades 4 - 6.

In eight fun-filled group sessions, your children will discover why such truths as honesty, justice, love, purity, self-control, mercy, and respect work to their best interests and how four simple steps will help them to make right moral choices an everyday habit.

Truth Works, Younger Children's Workbook ISBN 0-8054-9831-1
Truth Works, Older Children's Workbook ISBN 0-8054-9830-3
Truth Works, Leader's Guide ISBN 0-8054-9827-3

Contact your Christian supplier to help you obtain these "Right From Wrong" resources and begin to make it right in your home, your church, and your community.

Knowing
Right from Wrong

BIBLE VERSE

"Do what is right and good in the Lord's sight"
(Deuteronomy 6:18).

Session Goals

1. CONSIDER THE CHOICE:
   To teach children to consider their choices and to begin to use the Steps of Truth for making right choices

2. COMPARE IT TO GOD:
   To lead children to see what God is like and to ADMIT that we must compare our attitudes and actions to His perfect standard

3. COMMIT TO GOD'S WAY:
   To guide children to SUBMIT to God's way by being obedient to Him

4. COUNT ON GOD'S LOVING MOTIVATION
   TO PROTECT AND PROVIDE:
   To lead children to understand that God loves us and wants to provide for us and protect us; to be thankful for the benefits we enjoy when we make right choices

Leaders Need to Know

THE STEPS OF TRUTH
TO MAKE RIGHT CHOICES

Note: This material is a summary of Josh McDowell's book, **Right from Wrong.** *You are strongly encouraged to read this book as preparation to teach.*

Today's society no longer guides children to make right moral choices. Our culture with its emphasis on "value-free" education promotes a relative, "man-centered" view of truth. Consequently, many children have a distorted perception of how to determine right from wrong. Christian families must teach a new way of thinking about truth if we are going to reverse this trend. This program will help families to better do that. There are four simple Steps of Truth that we can teach to our children and use ourselves when faced with a moral choice. If learned and applied, these Steps of Truth can help children make right choices. Although we covered these steps in the introduction, we will recap them again. The four steps are:

STEP 1: CONSIDER the choice;
STEP 2: COMPARE it to God;
STEP 3: COMMIT to God's way; and
STEP 4: COUNT on God's protection and provision.

STEP 1: CONSIDER THE CHOICE:

In this first step we must ask: "What choices do I have and who determines what is right or wrong in this situation?"

This step erects a STOP sign of sorts to alert our children that their attitudes and actions are judged by someone other than themselves, and they are not to justify their behavior based on their own selfish interests.

Considering the choice creates a "Choice Conflict." The conflict is between making right choices and perhaps suffering some immediate negative consequences or making the wrong choices and enjoying some immediate "benefits." The conflict is between doing what we believe is in our short-term selfish interest or doing what God says is right in our long-term best interest.

STEP 2: COMPARE IT TO GOD:

At this step we ask: "Who determines what is right or wrong absolutely?" "How does this choice compare to God, the original standard?"

Here we acknowledge there is an absolute righteous God and that we must compare our attitudes and actions to Him and His words to determine whether they are right or wrong. This attitude, born out of a healthy fear of God, admits that there is an absolute standard that has already determined that certain things are **right for all people, for all times, for all places**. Absolute truth is objective, universal, and constant. God's written Word gives us specific and absolute guidelines regarding what is right and wrong. These guidelines, however, are not simply legalistic rules, but a reflection of the very nature and character of God Himself. When we compare our attitudes and actions to God, we ADMIT that His character and nature define right and wrong absolutely.

STEP 3: COMMIT TO GOD'S WAY:

Am I going to SUBMIT to God or choose my selfish way?

This is decision time. Once we have compared our selfish desires to God's absolute standard, we must choose between our way or God's way. When we commit to God's way, it means we turn from our selfishness and those attitudes and actions that are unlike Him. We SUBMIT to Him as Savior and Lord. This involves repentance, confession of sin, trusting Christ for forgiveness, and asking the Holy Spirit to fill us and empower us.

Ask:
What choices do you have and who determines what is right or wrong in this situation?

Admit:
That God's character and nature defines right and wrong absolutely.

Submit:
To God as Lord of our lives and rely on His power to live out His way in us.

Thank God:

For His loving protection and provision.

"Blessed are those who are persecuted because of righteousness, for theirs is the kingdom of heaven" (Matthew 5:10).

Provide:
☐ *Prepared name tags*
☐ *Markers*
☐ *Tape*

To Do:
☐ *Before the session, prepare name tags with blank space at the top for each child's name, followed by one of the following characteristics of God at the bottom:*

AMY
God is love

STEP 4: COUNT ON GOD'S LOVING MOTIVATION TO PROTECT AND PROVIDE:

Have I thanked God for His loving care?

Once we ADMIT God's sovereignty and SUBMIT to His authority, we can begin to see clearly the distinctions between right and wrong. We can also count on God's protection and provision. In this fourth step, we should thank God for this loving protection and provision. This does not mean we will not have trials. In fact, Jesus says that we may suffer for righteousness sake. But such suffering has great rewards. These include spiritual blessings like freedom from guilt, a clear conscience, the joy of sharing Christ, and most importantly, the loving approval of God in our lives. Moreover, we enjoy many physical, emotional, psychological, and relational benefits when we are obedient to God. A word of caution: God's protection and provision should not be our primary motivation to obey God. However, it certainly provides a powerful reinforcement for choosing right and rejecting wrong.

In summary, when considering a choice, I must compare my attitudes and actions to God, commit to His lordship, and count on His loving motivation to provide for me and protect me.

Truth Time

ACTIVITY (10 MINUTES)
WHAT IS GOD LIKE?

The purpose of this game is to lead children to discover seven truths about God.

As the children arrive, add their first names to the name tags above the line that describes who God is, without them seeing the name tag. Then place the name tags on their backs. Once the group has gathered, tell them they will be learning seven important things about God's nature and character—what He is like. For younger children, you may provide a list of the seven truths about God on a poster or chalkboard so they can ask yes and no questions and discover more easily what is on their name tag.

Instruct them to ask other children yes and no questions to try to discover the words or phrases on their name tags that tell us what God is like. Encourage children to take turns asking each other questions. They may only respond with yes or no. Once a child has discovered a characteristic of God on her name tag, the name tag may be moved from the back to the front. Then the child may continue to help others by answering yes or no questions.

When all of the children have identified what God is like, gather the children in a circle. Say: "These words on your name tags describe who God is. The Bible tells us that God is love, pure, true, just, mercy, the highest authority, and in control. God is perfect and always right. He is the one who defines what is right. We are going to learn how to make right choices based on what God is like. For example, God is true. If we choose to tell the truth, we know we are doing what is right."

God is love, God is pure, God is true, God is just, God is mercy, God is the highest authority, God is in control.

Study Group Time

(20 MINUTES)

1. Draw or write about the awesome things God has done.
   Say: "We can know more about what God is like by the wonderful things He has done. We are going to look at some of the things He has done." Direct the children's attention to the art paper. Explain that *awesome* means power that demands respect. Ask them to write or draw examples from the Bible of God's awesomeness. You may need to help young children think of stories such as the creation, Noah's ark, the Exodus, the Ten Commandments, David and Goliath, feeding the five thousand, Jesus healing the sick, and the resurrection. Give the children three to five minutes to write and draw the awesome things God has done.

2. Discuss the awesome things God has done.
   Ask the children to gather around the study group leader and sit in chairs or on the floor. Briefly discuss the events they have put on the wall. Emphasize how powerful and mighty God is. Say: "God has done many awesome and incredible things because He is a wonderful and awesome God. In other words, God is mighty, holy, powerful, wise, and loving. Because He is so awesome, we must have the greatest respect for Him."

3. Explain what *fear* means.
   Open your Bible and read Proverbs 1:7. Explain that fear does not mean being afraid of God because He is bad; but respecting Him because He is good. Therefore, we must obey God. Say: "Later in our discussion groups we will learn why it is important to fear or respect God. We will also learn how fearing God will help us make right choices."

Provide:
- [ ] *Art paper*
- [ ] *Tape*
- [ ] *Crayons*
- [ ] *Markers*

To Do:
- [ ] *Stretch art paper across one entire wall providing plenty of room for all of the children to write and draw. Write* **God Is Awesome Graffiti Wall** *in the center of the paper.*

"The fear of the Lord is the beginning of knowledge" (Proverbs 1:7).

Provide:

☐ *Poster paper or chalkboard*

To Do:

☐ *Write the following on a poster or chalkboard: "Do what is girth and doog in the Lord's sight" (Deuteronomy 6:18). Underline the jumbled words and leave room for children to write underneath the words.*

To Do:

☐ *Prepare a poster with the four steps or write the steps on the chalkboard.*

☐ *Be prepared! Practice the gestures that go with the four steps several times so that you will demonstrate them with confidence. Use the illustrations on page 33 if needed.*

4. Discover what God wants us to do.

Unscramble the words. Call the children's attention to the poster or chalkboard. Tell them you need help unscrambling words that describe what God wants us to do. Ask children to raise their hands if they can unscramble these words. Call on a child who has raised her hand and ask her to unscramble one word. If she says the correct word, ask her to write it under the scrambled word. If she says the wrong word, ask another child to help her. Use the same procedure for the other words.

5. Introduce the Steps of Truth.

Display a poster of the Steps of Truth. Say: "God really wants us to do what is right and good all the time. Sometimes doing right is easy, but sometimes it is difficult to do the right thing. During the next seven weeks, we are going to be learning a way to make right choices. The four Steps of Truth on this poster will help us with every choice we make. These steps will help us think and behave in ways that please God. This new way to make right choices has hand motions to help you remember the steps. Let me show you, and then you can do it with me." Show the hand motions and explain each step very briefly. (Group leaders will spend more time teaching the process in discussion time.)

STEP 1: CONSIDER THE CHOICE:

I have a choice to make. (Turn palms faceup and move hands alternately up and down.)

STEP 2: COMPARE IT TO GOD:

What does God say? When I do this, I am admitting that God is right. *Admit.* (Interlock hands as if in prayer with both index fingers pointed upward toward God.)

STEP 3: COMMIT TO GOD'S WAY:

When I do this, I am submitting to God based on who He is. *Submit.* (Point two thumbs up.)

STEP 4: COUNT ON GOD'S LOVING MOTIVATION TO PROTECT AND PROVIDE:

Because God loves me, He will protect me and provide for me when I choose to follow His way. *Result.* (Arch arms overhead like an umbrella.)

Invite the children to do the hand motions with you as you say the capitalized words.

6. Divide into small groups for discussion time.

Say: "We are going to break up into discussion groups and talk more about how to make right choices. You will be in the same group for the next seven weeks. Your group will do some fun activities and talk about how to make right choices." Divide the children by age into discussion groups of six.

Discussion Group Time

(30 MINUTES)

7. Get acquainted.

Give each child a *Truth Works* activity book. Use the first activity on page 5 as an icebreaker to help the children get to know the members of the group.

8. Focus on learning to make right choices.

Lead the children to turn to page 4 of *Truth Works*. Read and discuss this page. Lead the children to practice the hand motions for the Steps of Truth.

9. Ask, "Why should we fear God?"

Before you begin page 6 of *Truth Works*, tell the children that fearing God means to understand that God is holy. He is worthy of our respect and obedience. Fearing God does not mean being afraid of God because He is bad. Lead the children to work this activity as a group.

Older children can help others match the Scriptures to the reasons we fear God. Read the Scriptures out loud. Also ask older children to list by name or position six people they respect. Discuss the relationship of fear and respect.

Help younger children circle the correct answers. Use the activity as an opportunity to discuss how great God is and how we should fear (respect and obey) Him.

10. Copy the Original.

This activity will encourage children to compare their actions to God and not others. Give each child a blank sheet of paper. Use a sheet of paper and draw a geometric shape. Color the shape. Show the children the colored shape. Tell them they have 30 seconds to look at the design, and then they will copy it on their papers. Place your original copy in the center and then remove it. Give them time to color their designs. Encourage individual work.

After they have finished coloring, ask them to return to the table. Let

Provide:
☐ **Truth Works** *activity books*
☐ *Tables for each group*
☐ *Pencils*
☐ *Markers or crayons*

Answers to page 6:
Older Children—
1-D; 2-A; 3-B; 4-C
Younger Children—
obey him, look up to him, listen to him, honor him

Provide:
☐ *Crayons or markers in three colors*
☐ *Blank paper*

To Do:
☐ *Color several geometric designs. Use three colors for each child. (For example, if you*

*have six children, you
will need six red, six
blue, and six yellow.)
Option: If you do
not have enough of the
same colors for each
child, use a pencil and
draw lines, circles,
and solid shading in
the design for them
to copy.*

*"Be perfect, therefore,
as your heavenly Father is
perfect" (Matthew 5:48).*

*Note: Allow time for
discussion. Remember
to listen!*

Important:

*As you go through the
spelling test example, ask
for the children's input.
Get them involved in the
thought process!*

them compare their designs to see how they are alike and different. Ask, "Who thinks your design is exactly right?" Then place the original copy in the center and let them compare their copies. Help each child see how his or her drawing compares to the original. Ask, "Now who thinks your copy is exactly right?" Say: "We know it is right if it is just like the original. God wants us to compare our behavior to Him. He is the original."

11. What the Bible says about doing what God does.
    Ask a child to read Matthew 5:48.
    Ask, "To whom should we compare our choices?" Discuss how right choices are made and who helps you make choices. Use this discussion as a chance to review. Say: "We have already seen how awesome God is from who He is (name tag game) and the wonderful things He has done (on the art paper). When we have to make a choice, it is important to look at what God says and what He is like. He is the original. God is awesome. He loves you and wants the very best for you. When you make right choices, you can count on God to provide for you and protect you."

12. Practice the Steps of Truth.
    Lead the children to turn again to page 4 in *Truth Works*. Look at the Steps of Truth chart on the lower half of the page. Review the hand motions and talk about each step. Tell the children: "During the next seven weeks, we will be learning how to make right choices. We want to help you know how to choose God's way. This new way of making right choices will help you for the rest of your life. Let's use an example to show how this new way works."

SPELLING TEST CASE STUDY

Imagine that you have a spelling test at school. You do not know how to spell one of the words. The teacher steps out of the room. The boy next to you always makes a 100 on spelling tests. You could see his paper if you wanted to look.

STEP 1: CONSIDER THE CHOICE:
You know if you cheat, you will get a better grade. If you do not cheat, you will get a lower grade. Your parents will give you five dollars if you get a higher grade. You really want the money. How do you choose what is right? *(Leader: The more you emphasize the choice conflict of truth or better grade, the more they will understand why they always need to turn from their selfish ways to make right, moral choices.)*

STEP 2: COMPARE IT TO GOD:

God has given us a rule, "Do not deceive one another" (Leviticus 19:11). Why is being honest right? *(God is true.)* He can never be dishonest or cheat. You must compare your action to God to know what is right. God is the original standard for what is right.

STEP 3: COMMIT TO GOD'S WAY:

Choose God's way. God is true, and you love and fear God. Therefore, you must turn from the temptation to get a higher grade and do the right thing.

STEP 4: COUNT ON GOD'S LOVING MOTIVATION TO PROTECT AND PROVIDE:

Provide:
☐ *Umbrella*

God loves you and wants the very best for you. God protects and provides for you when you choose His way. Umbrellas provide dry shelter and protect you from getting wet (take out unopened umbrella). When you do not commit to God's way, you are not under His protection. However, when you choose God's way, He provides for you and protects you (open umbrella and place it over your head).

Refusing to cheat will protect you from feeling guilty. Choosing not to cheat will keep you from forming a pattern of cheating, repeating the same dishonest act again and again. Not cheating will keep you from a bad relationship with your teacher, classmates, parents, and God. Choosing not to cheat will provide you with a clear conscience, a sense of pride in your own work, a good reputation, and the trust of others. Just as this umbrella protects you from the rain, God protects you when you make right choices. You can thank God for His protection.

13. Introduce the daily assignments.

    Remove the assignment sheets from each child's *Truth Works*. Distribute the assignment sheets. Briefly go over the assignments for the week. Explain that every Monday they are to memorize the verse that has been chosen for the session. This week, the verse is short: "Do what is right and good in the Lord's sight" (Deuteronomy 6:18). Say: "One of the reasons we have put the memory verse as the first thing you do is that we want you to remember the verse all week. Repeat it to yourself every time you have a chance to do right or wrong."

    Provide:
    ☐ *Daily assignment sheets from* **Truth Works**

14. Distribute the *Truth Works Journal*.

    Say: "For the next seven weeks we are going to be talking about making right choices. Use this journal to write the choices you have each week and how you used the Steps of Truth to make your choices."

    Provide:
    ☐ *Copies of the* **Truth Works Journal** *(see pages 35-36)*

15. Pray.

Lead in prayer or ask a volunteer to pray. Dismiss the children.

RIGHT *FROM* WRONG®

Honesty
God Is True

BIBLE VERSE

"Do not steal. Do not lie. Do not deceive one another. Do not swear falsely.
Do not defraud your neighbor or rob him"
(Leviticus 19:11-13).

Session Goals

1. CONSIDER THE CHOICE:
   To lead children to consider which choice is right or wrong regarding God's commands to be honest by: (a) telling the truth (not lying); (b) respecting other people's things (not stealing); and (c) doing one's own work (not cheating)

2. COMPARE IT TO GOD:
   To lead children to ADMIT that we must compare our attitudes and actions to God's standard of honesty because God is true

3. COMMIT TO GOD'S WAY:
   To lead children to SUBMIT to God's way by being obedient to God's commands to be honest

4. COUNT ON GOD'S LOVING MOTIVATION
   TO PROTECT AND PROVIDE:
   To lead children to thank God for His loving motivation to provide for us and protect us which comes as a result of being honest

Leaders Need to Know

This material is taken from Josh McDowell's book, Right from Wrong, pages 167-181.

The 1994 Churched Youth survey revealed that youth struggle with honesty. In a three month time period:

66 percent lied to a parent or teacher.

59 percent lied to a friend or peer.

36 percent cheated on an exam.

15 percent stole money or other possessions.

The youth in our churches are acting dishonestly because they have embraced a "man-centered" view of truth. They are buying into a notion that lying and cheating are legitimate ways to get ahead. If we are going to help our children make consistently honest choices, we must help them develop a "God-centered" view of truth. We must help children learn to choose to be honest.

PRECEPT

See:

*Achan's sin—Joshua 7
Annanias and
Sapphira— Acts 5:1-11*

God has given many commands in His Word regarding truth. In the Ten Commandments given to Moses, God makes it clear that lying, cheating, and stealing are wrong. Throughout the Bible God repeats these truths and punishes dishonesty severely (e.g. Achan, Annanias and Sapphira).

PRINCIPLE

Honesty is the positive principle behind the negative (Thou shalt NOT) commands against lying, stealing, and cheating. Honesty is the quality of being truthful, transparent, and trustworthy. An honest person will not lie, cheat, or steal.

PERSON

God is true. Truth comes from His nature, and anything contrary to God's nature is sin. Honesty is right (and dishonesty is wrong) because God is true. Therefore, lying, cheating, and stealing are offenses against God's nature. God's character is true, so honesty is right for all people, for all times, and for all places.

GOD'S LOVING MOTIVATION TO PROTECT AND PROVIDE

God's standards of honesty:
1. Protects from guilt.
   Provides for a clear conscience.
2. Protects from shame.
   Provides for a sense of accomplishment.
3. Protects from the cycle of deceit.
   Provides for a reputation of integrity.
4. Protects from ruined relationships.
   Provides for trusting relationships.

Truth Time

ACTIVITY (10 MINUTES) "STEAL THE ERASER"

The purpose of this activity is to introduce the concepts of cheating, stealing, and lying.

As children arrive, greet them and help them put on name tags. Once a small group has gathered (about six), divide the children into two equal teams. Number each team beginning with number one. Lead the teams to face each other, seated in two straight lines that are at least twelve feet apart. Say: "We

See:
Joshua 7:11,
Acts 5:3-4

See:
Ephesians 4:25,
1 Corinthians 6:10,
Titus 2:10

See:
Deuteronomy 32:4,
Titus 1:2, Hebrews 6:18,
Romans 3:4

Provide:
☐ *Name tags*
☐ *Markers*
☐ *Eraser*

To Do:
☐ *Prepare an adult scorekeeper in advance for a "cheating" role with these instructions:*
1. *When one team gets to seven points, give the team that is behind two points instead of one.*
2. *The very next round, run out and steal the*

eraser and take it back to the board. Add your own name and a point. When the children react, deny cheating on the score, taking the eraser, or doing anything wrong.

are going to play 'Steal the Eraser.' When I call out a number, the players with that number will each race to the center and try to steal the eraser. The one who grabs the eraser must get back to her spot before the player from the other team can take her spot. If you steal the eraser and get back to your spot first, your team gets a point. The first team to get ten points wins." With larger groups, you may call out more than one number at a time.

As the game progresses, make sure your adult scorekeeper performs the special dishonest role (see note in column). Allow the children to react to the cheating of the scorekeeper. Finish the game and gather the children in a large circle.

Study Group Time

(20 MINUTES)

1. Ask the following questions:
   - Did you see the scorekeeper do anything wrong?
     (He was cheating, stealing, and lying.)
   - Did the scorekeeper do his job fairly?
     (No, he changed the score.)
   - Did the scorekeeper respect other people's things?
     (No, he stole the eraser.)
   - Did the scorekeeper tell the truth about his actions?
     (No, he said he did not change the score or take the eraser.)
   - What was wrong with his actions?
     (Cheating, lying, and stealing are dishonest and wrong.)
     IMPORTANT: Tell the children that the scorekeeper is not a dishonest person. Inform them that you had asked him to play the role of a dishonest scorekeeper in order to get them to think about honesty.

2. Introduce honesty as the topic for the day.
   Say: "Today we are going to learn why honesty is right for all people, for all places, for all times. God is true, so we should be true and honest. Honesty includes many things like telling the truth, respecting other people's things, and doing one's own work. It may be easier for you to think about what truth or honesty will not do. Truth will not lie, steal, or cheat. God has spoken clearly about this in His Word."

Provide:
☐ *NIV Bible*
☐ *God's NOT Poster*

3. Read what God has said about being honest.

    Call on someone to read Leviticus 19:11-13.

    Ask all of the children to listen for things God has said not to do. Ask the children to fill in "God's NOT List" on the chalkboard or poster you made.

    Explain the following:

    > *Steal*—to take something that is not yours
    >
    > *Lie*—to purposely say something that is not true
    >
    > *Deceive one another*—to trick or mislead someone into believing a lie
    >
    > *Swear falsely*—make a promise that is not true or a promise that you do not keep
    >
    > *Defraud your neighbor*—cheat your neighbor out of something that is his
    >
    > *Rob*—wrongly take something from your neighbor

    Say: "All of these things are dishonest. We should not do them because our true God will not do them. God will not lie, steal, or cheat. Let's look at some events from the Bible that show that God is honest, and He keeps His promises."

4. Draw or act out Bible events that show God is true and honest.

    Divide the children into three equal groups. Tell them you are going to give each group a Bible event to act out or draw on the board. The events all show God is true. The other teams will have to guess what is being acted or drawn. The teams may choose to act and/or draw, but they may not speak. Whisper the descriptions to one member on each team. Ask them to split into different parts of the room to secretly discuss how they will act and draw their event.

    TEAM A: Draw and/or act God bringing Israel out of Egyptian slavery and parting the Red Sea for them to cross.

    TEAM B: Draw and/or act God giving a rainbow after Noah and the ark survived the flood.

    TEAM C: Draw and/or act Jesus taking a little boy's lunch of five loaves and two fish, blessing it, and feeding 5,000 with twelve baskets left.

    Give each team a few minutes to discuss how they will draw or act. Then ask Team A to go first while the other teams guess. After the teams guess the crossing of the Red Sea, ask someone to read Exodus 6:6-8. Ask: "What did God promise?" (*to take Israel out of Egypt and give them the promised land*) "Was He true to His promise?" (*yes*) Ask someone else to read Joshua 21:43-45. Stress that God does not lie, but keeps His promis-

---

To Do:

God's "NOT" list

1. Do not _____.

2. Do not _____.

3. Do not _____ one another.

4. Do not _____.

5. Do not _____ your neighbor or _____ him.

To Do:

☐ *Tell adult leaders to be ready to help each of the three groups. You may want to write each team's event on note cards so that they can read them as well as hear them.*

Provide:

☐ *NIV Bible with book markers at: Exodus 6:6-8; Joshua 21:43-45; Genesis 9:11-13; John 6:5-13*

es. Keep discussion brief and use only enough of the story to show that God is true.

Let Team B go next. After the children guess the answer *(the rainbow)*, ask: "Why did God flood the world?" *(because the people were wicked)* "What was God's plan to save Noah's family and the animals?" *(the ark)* "What did the rainbow represent?" *(God's promise to never destroy the earth with a flood again)* Ask a child to read Genesis 9:11-13. Say: "God has kept His promise. While there have been regional floods, there has never been a flood that destroyed the whole world since Noah's time."

Ask Team C to go next. After the children guess the answer *(the feeding of the five thousand)*, read John 6:5-13. Ask: "Did Jesus steal the boy's lunch?" *(No, the boy offered his lunch.)* "Did Jesus return the lunch?" *(Yes, not only was the boy able to eat lunch, but more than five thousand other people ate.)* Say: "Jesus shows us what God is like. God is honest; He does not steal."

5. Dismiss the children to their assigned discussion groups.

Discussion Group Time

(30 MINUTES)

Provide:

☐ *Truth Works*

☐ *Pencils*

☐ *Magnet*

Swear falsely—*make a promise that is not true or a promise that you do not keep*

Defraud your neighbor—*cheat your neighbor out of something that is his*

6. Introduce the topic—Honesty.

Distribute *Truth Works* and pens or pencils to the children.

Instruct the children to turn to page 7. Lead them to read and work through the page.

As you go over the Bible verses, Leviticus 19:11-13 (for younger children only verse 11), make sure you help the older children understand what *swear falsely* and *defraud* mean. These terms are not a part of their vocabulary.

Provide a large magnet that is marked with the positive and negative ends. Explain that while a magnet has two different fields of power, it is still one magnet. Both sides of the magnet will pick up the paper clips. Yes, both sides get the same job done, but they do it with different charges of magnetic power. One charge is positive and the other is negative. The same is true about God's law. Each time God instructs us not to do something in a negative way, He is also telling us to do something positive. Both the negative command and the positive principle teach us what God is like and what He wants us to be like. Call attention to the two lists on the bottom of page 7.

7. Review and teach the Steps of Truth.

Children who were present last week may be able to recall the Steps of Truth. Since this is only session two, do not assume they will remember the Steps of Truth. Take time to go through the steps and explain again what each of them means, especially if your group has children that were not present last week. Lead the children to use the hand motions. Use the material in session one for review if needed. Call attention to the chart you made of the Steps of Truth. The chart should read:

Steps of Truth

STEP 1: CONSIDER the choice.

STEP 2: COMPARE our attitudes and actions to God's.

STEP 3: CHOOSE God's way.

STEP 4: COUNT on God's protection and provision.

Provide:
☐ *Poster board*
☐ *Marker*

To Do:
☐ *Make a poster of the Steps of Truth*

8. Apply the Steps of Truth.

Guide the children to turn to page 8 in *Truth Works*. Lead the children to use the Steps of Truth to determine the outcome of each case. Leaders, the cases and information below will help you as you lead in discussion. Older children will have three case studies. Younger children will work through cases two and three.

CASE 1

"I, Jeremy, the defendant, had two weeks to do a book report for school. I put off reading the book and played with my friends instead. The night before the book report was due, I realized there wasn't enough time to read the book and do the report. I remembered there was a movie about the book. If I rented the movie and watched it, I could make the report."

STEP 1: CONSIDER THE CHOICE:

Leaders, the choice conflict stated in the first person is:

(1) "If I don't make the report, I will get a failing grade."

(2) "I know I was supposed to read the book, but if I watch the movie and do the report from it, I might even get an A. How do I make the right choice?"

STEP 2: COMPARE OUR ATTITUDES AND ACTIONS TO GOD:

Ask: "What does God say?"

Ask a child to read the Bible verses for today, Leviticus 19:11-13. Ask, "Which part of these Bible verses will help Jeremy know what choice is the right choice?" (*"Do not lie. Do not deceive one another."*)

Note: Children may think if they do not tell a teacher they have not read the book assignment, then they have not lied. Explain that a person

"Do not steal. Do not lie. Do not deceive one another. Do not swear falsely . . . Do not defraud your neighbor or rob him" (*Leviticus 19:11-13*).

can also tell a lie by not telling the truth or presenting something as truth that is not exactly the truth. That is what the Bible means when it says, "Do not deceive one another."

Ask, "Does Jeremy have any other choices?" Lead the children to understand that Jeremy could use what time he has to read the book. He could honestly tell his teacher how far he read and ask her if he could turn in his report late. Point out that he will have to accept the teacher's answer and the consequences of whatever the teacher chooses.

STEP 3: COMMIT TO GOD'S WAY

Lead the children to identify which choice would please God in this situation. Children may rationalize that it would please God and their parents for them to make good grades. Be sure and explain why the way we choose to make good grades is even more important than the grades. Then say: "For Jeremy to make the right choice, he must admit he was selfish in playing with his friends rather than doing his book report. He must turn from his selfish ways, accept the consequences, and commit to God's way."

STEP 4: COUNT ON GOD'S LOVING MOTIVATION
TO PROTECT AND PROVIDE:

Ask, "How will God protect and provide for Jeremy if he chooses to tell his teacher the truth?" Since this is only the second session, you may have to help the children identify God's protection and provisions. If the children cannot come up with these, say: "God will protect Jeremy from guilt and provide him with a clear conscience. God will protect him from being deceitful and provide him with a good reputation. God will protect him from the consequences of being caught cheating and provide him with the peace that comes from telling the truth."

CASE 2

"I, Kelly, the defendant, and my friend were really thirsty and we only had enough money for one can of soda. I put the money in the soda machine. A can came out and our money came back in the coin return.

STEP 1: CONSIDER THE CHOICE:

Leaders, the choice conflict for Kelly is:

(1) "Wow, was I lucky or what? I could use the money to buy my friend a can of soda. We are both so thirsty. After all, it was not our fault the machine made a mistake!"

(2) "I could return the money to the people who own the soda machine, but my friend and I will have to share one soda. We really want our own cans. How do I make the right choice?"

STEP 2: COMPARE IT TO GOD:

What does God say?

Ask the children, "Which part of our memory verses today will help Kelly know what to do?" *("Do not steal.")*

Note: Some children may not think that keeping extra money from a machine is stealing. They may rationalize that they were not trying to steal. After all, just think of all the times the machines keep our money! Help them understand that each time we take or use money that is not ours, we have stolen it from someone else.

STEP 3: COMMIT TO GOD'S WAY:

Lead children to tell you which choice would please God in this situation. Ask them to tell you why they think it would please God. Help them to understand that God is always honest. To be honest Kelly must turn from her selfish ways and commit to God's way.

STEP 4: COUNT ON GOD'S LOVING MOTIVATION TO PROTECT AND PROVIDE:

Ask: "How will God protect and provide for Kelly if she chooses to honor God and return the money to the people who own the soda machine?"

CASE 3

"I, Carlos, the defendant, was staying at home with my older sister. Our parents asked us to clean the house while they ran errands for three hours. After my parents left, I watched TV while my older sister cleaned the house. When my parents came home, they said: 'Thank you both for making the house so beautiful. We are going to take you for ice cream for doing all this hard work.' My older sister glared at me but didn't say anything although she had done all the work."

STEP 1: CONSIDER THE CHOICE:

Leaders, the choice conflict for Carlos is:

(1) "If I say nothing, my sister probably won't tell on me, and I'll get to go for ice cream."

(2) "If I confess I did not help clean the house, my parents might not buy me ice cream. I really want some. There are times I have covered for my sister, so what difference could it make? How do I make the right choice?"

STEP 2: COMPARE IT TO GOD:

Ask, "What does God say?"

Say: "Look again at today's Bible verses. How can these verses help Carlos know what to do?" *("Do not lie. Do not deceive one another.")* Say: "Because God is true and honest, He has commanded us to be true and honest. If Carlos keeps silent, he is deceiving his parents and not obeying God's commandment."

STEP 3: COMMIT TO GOD'S WAY:

Lead the children to tell you which choice would please God in this situation. Ask them to tell you why they think it will please God. Ask, "What does Carlos have to do to make the right choice?" *(Carlos must turn from his selfish desire to have ice cream that he did not earn. He must commit to God's way and be honest.)*

STEP 4: COUNT ON GOD'S LOVING MOTIVATION
TO PROTECT AND PROVIDE:

Ask the children to tell you how God protects and provides for the child who obeys Him and is honest.

Provide:

☐ *Truth Works*

☐ *Pencils*

Note: Take time to explain benefits *and* consequences

9. Apply the Steps of Truth to a personal experience.

Ask the children to turn to page 9. This activity is designed to lead the children to identify a true-life temptation to be dishonest that they have faced or could face in the future. Essentially, they will be writing their own case studies and continuing to learn to apply the Steps of Truth to the situations they identify. If time permits, let the children share their situations and tell how the Steps of Truth can help them make the right choices.

10. Practice being honest.

The purpose of this activity is to help children practice discerning when a person is choosing to be honest or dishonest. You will not have time to go through the Steps of Truth on each situation. The children have already gone through two or more case studies and have identified one of their own life situations.

Instruct the children to turn to pages 10 and 11 in *Truth Works*. Older children will have 10 situations to consider, and younger children will study 6 situations. Ask the children to read the situations on these two pages. Instruct them to write on the line next to each situation **h** for honest, **l** for lying, **c** for cheating, or **s** for stealing. Should time permit or all the children in the group miss a particular item, discuss the Steps of Truth as they relate to the particular situation.

The situations and their answers are:

S 1. Your parent sent you to the store with $10.00. The bill was $9.65. You kept the extra 35 cents because you felt you deserved the change for your effort. *(Younger Pupil # 1)*

H 2. You are riding your bike with your friends. You all start playing "wipe out" to see how close you can come to parked cars without hitting them. You go too fast and crash into the side of a car, leaving scratches and a dent. You tell the owner what you have done.

L 3. You ask your parents if you can go to the library for two hours. You go to the library for 1 hour and 45 minutes and the video arcade for 15 minutes. When your parents ask how your trip to the library was, you say: "Fine. I checked out two new books." *(Younger Pupil # 2)*

H 4. You go to use the pay phone at your school. When you deposit your quarter, several quarters come out the return slot. You take all the quarters and return them to the principal's office. *(Younger Pupil # 3)*

C 5. Your teacher has you exchange papers for grading. Your classmate overlooks the only wrong answer on your paper. You turn it in as a perfect grade.

H 6. You are playing a board game with your family and you are keeping score. Your sister almost has the 100 points needed to win. You have 94 points and earn five more. As scorekeeper, you could stretch your score to 100, but you remain honest and let your sister win the game. *(Younger Pupil # 4)*

L 7. You go to the carnival on your 10th birthday. Ride tickets are $1.00 for ages two to nine and $2.00 for ages ten and up. You tell the ticket seller that you are nine to get the lower price. *(Younger Pupil # 5. Ages are changed for younger.)*

C 8. Your team is one run behind in a baseball game. You hit a long ball over the left fielder's head. You run so fast around the bases trying to get home that you miss third base. The umpire doesn't notice and counts your run as good. You don't say anything and let the run count.

_H_ 9. Your teacher asks everyone to work quietly in their seats while she leaves the room for five minutes. You and two other classmates run around the room. When the teacher comes back, she says, "Those who did not stay in their seats, please raise your hands." You raise your hand and have to stay in at recess. *(Younger Pupil # 6)*

_S_ 10. You are at your best friend's house and notice that he has a really neat set of colored markers. You tell him you wish you had some markers like that. He says: "Here, you may have them. I'll get some more from the art cabinet at school." You don't want to lose your best friend so you take the markers.

Provide:

☐ *Daily Assignments*

11. Distribute the daily assignments.

Ask the children to report on how well they did on the daily assignments of the previous week. If time permits, ask if anyone remembers the memory verse for last week. Say, "One of the the things that can help us make the right choices in life is to know by memory some of the Bible verses that tell us what God wants us to do." Say some words of encouragement for those children who did the daily assignments. Encourage the ones who did not do the assignments to try and do them this week.

Distribute the assignment sheets you removed from *Truth Works* before the session. Go over the daily assignments for the coming week.

12. Dismiss the children with prayer.

Ask God to help us remember to honor Him by choosing to be honest with ourselves and others this week.

Purity
God Is Pure

"Do you not know that your body is a temple of the Holy Spirit, who is in you, whom you have received from God? You are not your own; you were bought at a price. Therefore **honor God with your body**"
(1 Corinthians 6:19-20).

Session Goals

1. CONSIDER THE CHOICE:
   To lead children to consider which choice is right or wrong regarding God's commands to honor God with our bodies which is to live pure

2. COMPARE IT TO GOD:
   To lead children to ADMIT that we must compare our attitudes and actions to God's standard of purity because God is pure

3. COMMIT TO GOD'S WAY:
   To lead children to SUBMIT to a pure God by being obedient to God's commands to live pure

4. COUNT ON GOD'S LOVING MOTIVATION
   TO PROTECT AND PROVIDE:
   To lead children to thank God for His loving motivation to provide for us and protect us that comes as a result of being obedient to a pure God

Leaders Need to Know

The material presented in this session is found in chapter 10, of **Right From Wrong** *"What's the Truth about Sex?" The application of this lesson for children will not extend to sexual behavior; however, it will be helpful for you to review chapter 10, pages 147-166, for you to gain understanding of this biblical principle.*

Our children today are increasingly being influenced by a "perverse and crooked" generation. Children need only to watch an evening of prime time television to be bombarded with messages of violence, unwholesome language, illicit drugs, and sexual immorality. How do we counter the culture and teach our children to honor God with their bodies in thought, word, and deed?

We can begin by teaching our children what it means to be pure (free from anything dirty or hurtful; clear, unadulterated, virtuous, and just). Children need to know that God is pure. They need to understand that we honor God with our bodies when we choose to keep our thoughts clean, our language decent, and our actions moral. While this lesson is not designed to teach children specifically about sexual morality, it will teach the foundational principle of purity that can be applied to sexual issues in their lives in years to come.

PRECEPTS

God's plan is for us to honor our bodies because it is with our bodies that we worship Him. We sing His praise with our mouths and pray with our minds. The Bible tells us God's Holy Spirit lives in a Christian's body. First

Corinthians 6:19-20 is the Scripture to memorize for this session. These verses teach the biblical precept of purity.

PRINCIPLE

God's command to honor Him with our bodies is based on the biblical principle of purity. In this session we will focus on purity. Purity begins with our thoughts and extends to our outward actions. Therefore, we must teach children to keep their thoughts and actions pure.

PERSON

The principle of purity is right because it reflects the nature of God. God is pure. When a person commits an immoral act, he violates the very nature of who God is.

GOD'S LOVING MOTIVATION TO PROTECT AND PROVIDE

Choosing God's standards for pure moral behavior offers us the following protections and provisions:
1. Protects us from guilt.
   Provides us with spiritual rewards.
2. Protects us from impure thoughts.
   Provides us with clean thinking patterns.

We can help children accept the truth that God made our bodies special. They can learn that God expects us to care for and respect our bodies. We are also to respect the bodies of others. The principle of purity includes honoring God with what we see and what we say.

Truth Time

ACTIVITY (10 MINUTES) "HAZARDOUS WASTE POND"

The purpose of this activity is to introduce the concept of purity in contrast to being contaminated or impure.

Greet the children as they arrive. Use name tags if the children are unfamiliar with each other.

Provide:
- [ ] *Self-adhesive name tags*
- [ ] *Tape*
- [ ] *Pins*
- [ ] *Pens or markers*
- [ ] *Blue art paper*
- [ ] *Brown or red construction paper*
- [ ] *Other colors of construction paper*

To Do:
- [ ] *Ask at least three children to remain pure.*
- [ ] *On bright-colored half sheets of paper write* **Contaminated.**
- [ ] *On construction paper write* **Environmental Protection Supervisors.**
- [ ] *Tape the blue art paper to the floor. Create a narrow path through the center of the "pond" with a contrasting color of construction paper or with masking tape. Make the bridge difficult to cross without touching the water, but not impossible. Using brown construction paper, cut out splotches of various shapes. On one side of each splotch write* **Pollution** *or* **Hazardous Waste.** *On the other side write one of the following*

77

phrases: **illegal drugs, dirty movies, bad words, lying, cheating, mean thoughts, getting drunk, disobeying parents, stealing.** *Tape the splotches to the blue art paper. The splotches should have the words* **Pollution** *or* **Hazardous Waste** *facing up.*

Children are knowledgeable of environmental issues because environmental themes are a part of Saturday morning cartoons and "green issues" are covered in their school curriculum.

Inform the children that they are to walk on the bridge that crosses the center of the "pond" without getting contaminated by falling into the water or stepping off the bridge. The leaders should wear name tags that designate them as "Environmental Protection Supervisors." If you can easily get hard hats, the leaders should wear them.

Leaders should have tags that say *contaminated* to tape on each child who steps off the bridge into the "pond." When a child gets contaminated, the leaders need to help her out of the *water* and label her *contaminated.* The children will have fun watching others make the walk. There will be some children who will purposely become contaminated. Remember you are working with children. Have fun and enjoy them!

Study Group Time

Provide:

☐ *Items with the word pure on the label*
☐ *Poster board*
☐ *Dictionary*

To Do:

☐ *Make a poster with the definition of pure.*

Pure——Not mixed with anything else. Not containing anything dirty or hurtful, clear. Not bad or evil; virtuous, innocent, or just.

1. Talk about *pure.*
   Before the session gather items that advertise being pure. Ask the children to bring their chairs to the study group area. They should form a single semicircle around the Study Leader. Children who are *contaminated,* however, must sit on one side of the semicircle and the *pure* children on the other side. A leader or "Environmental Protection Supervisor" must sit between the two groups to provide protection for the *pure* group. If possible sit near or around the pond.
   Call attention to the display of items that have the word *pure* on them. For example, use pure vanilla extract, pure cane sugar, pure honey, pure orange juice, pure soap, pure olive oil, or pure ground pepper.
   Ask the children to look over the items displayed and find the one word they have in common. They should discover that all the items claim to be pure.
   Ask, "Why do you think the word *pure* is important to each of these products?" *(These products do not have any other ingredients mixed with them except the one that is listed. The product is clean or not contaminated.)*

2. Define pure.
   If possible have a copy of a children's dictionary available. Ask a *pure* child to look up the word *pure* and read the definition to the group. Make a poster with the definition. Call attention to the poster.

The children may have some interesting variations of this definition. Discuss their answers.

3. Transition to biblical truth.

   Say: "These products fit part of the definition for *pure* on our poster. Which part of the definition is not covered?" *(clear, not bad or evil; virtuous, innocent, or just)*

   Say: "While these products claim to be pure in some ways, we learn from the Bible that God is pure in every way. Today we are going to talk about the truth that God is pure."

4. Present the truth about purity.

   Ask a leader to read 1 John 3:3. Tell the following stories.

   God is pure and perfect in every way. When God created the world, He created a special garden in which people could live. We call that place the garden of Eden. The garden was perfect and pure. The first two people God created were Adam and Eve. They were created to be pure. One sad day Adam and Eve sinned against God. They did the one thing God told them they should not do. That is how impure sin came into the world. Because Adam and Eve were no longer pure, God could not allow them to live in the pure garden of Eden. God still loved them, and He provided another place for them to live.

   God continued to want to teach people that He was pure. One day God spoke to Moses in a special way. God used a burning bush to get Moses' attention. The bush was on fire, but it was not burning. Moses went to the bush to take a closer look. He heard God's voice. "Do not come any closer," God said. "Take off your sandals, for the place where you are standing is holy ground" (Exodus 3:5). God wanted Moses to understand that He was holy and pure. God was teaching Moses that he was in a pure place because God Himself was there.

   God had a very special job for Moses. God wanted Moses to rescue His people from slavery in Egypt. After the Israelite people escaped Egypt, they spent a long time following God through the desert. God was using this time in their lives to teach them about who He was. One lesson God wanted to teach His people was that He was pure.

   One day God told Moses to tell all the Israelite people to bring Him an offering. The offering was to be used to build a special place to worship God. This place was called the tabernacle. The Israelites were instructed to go to the tabernacle to learn about and worship God. Today we come to our church building to learn about God and worship Him like the Israelites went to the tabernacle.

God had some clear directions for this offering. First, the offering was to be given freely. The people were only to give God what they wanted to give Him. God wanted them to give the offering because they loved Him and wanted to obey Him. Secondly, the offering was to be from the finest items the people had. God wanted the tabernacle to represent the best the people had to offer because it was a very special place to remind them of God. After they took the offering, God said, "Then have them make a sanctuary for me, and I will dwell among them. Make this tabernacle and all its furnishings exactly like the pattern I will show you" (Exodus 25:8-9).

Gold is a metal that can be made pure. God commanded that the most important things in His tabernacle be made of pure gold. God wanted the people to make a gold chest in which to place the Ten Commandments. We call this chest the ark of the covenant. Two golden angels were to be on top of the chest. God required pure gold to be used to make the altar where sacrifices were offered to Him. He instructed the craftsmen to design a golden table and ten golden lamp stands, lamps, and other golden items. God even wanted the door sockets to be made of pure gold. He did this so that when the people entered the tabernacle to worship God they would see all the pure gold and remember that God was pure.

5. Apply Bible truths.
Say: "Because God is pure, He wants us to be pure. God cares for us more than we could ever care for ourselves. God made our bodies very special, and He values our bodies. What we do with our minds and bodies is important to God, after all, He made us!"

Say: "The pond you had to cross when you first came into the room had pollution in it which caused it to be impure. We told you the pollution was hazardous waste. What are some of the ways we can pollute our bodies and minds?" *(taking illegal drugs, seeing dirty movies, using bad words, lying, cheating, stealing, thinking hateful things about others)*

Lead the children to stand on the banks of the pond. Turn over the brown splotches. Read the various pollutants that can contaminate our lives.

6. Lead in prayer.
While standing around the polluted pond, say: "God is pure. He does not want any of these pollutants to harm us. God is also merciful and will forgive us when we admit we have chosen the wrong way. We can change our attitudes and ask Him to forgive us."

Lead the children in prayer. Ask God to help us look to Him when we have to make choices. Ask Him to help us remember who He is so that we can choose to make the right choices about how we treat our bodies and the bodies of others.

Say, "When God forgives us, He removes the contamination from our lives, and we can have fellowship with Him again." As you say this, the leaders should be removing the contamination signs from the children who are wearing them. Dismiss the children to their small discussion groups.

Discussion Group Time

(30 MINUTES)

7. Use *Truth Works.*
Distribute *Truth Works* and lead the children to turn to page 12. Ask four volunteers to read the four paragraphs on this page. Use the lower half of the page to review the definition of *pure.* Ask the children to fill in the blanks at the bottom of the page.

8. Use the Bible verses.
Call attention to 1 Corinthians 6:19-20 on page 13 of *Truth Works.*

For leaders of older children
Give the older children time to write their answers to the questions based on this verse.
Discuss their answers. The questions and possible answers are as follows:
- How is the body like a temple?
(We worship God in a temple, we worship God with our bodies. God dwelt in the Old Testament temple, the Holy Spirit dwells in us.)
- Why is it important to keep a temple clean?
(The temple is where we worship God. Our bodies belong to God.)
- Why should we want to be pure?
(God is pure.)
- What does God want us to do with our bodies?
(God wants us to honor Him with our bodies.)

For leaders of younger children
Lead younger children to study the same Scripture. Suggest that they use the space provided to draw a picture of how they can honor or worship God.

9. Apply the Steps of Truth.
Use these case studies to stimulate further thinking and practice the Steps of Truth. Simply read these aloud or print them on cards for the children to read.

Provide:
- [ ] *Truth Works*
- [ ] *Pencils and crayons or markers*

CASE 1

Last weekend you went on a camping trip with a bunch of guys from your school. While the leaders were setting up camp and unloading the gear, some of the guys in your group huddled around a magazine that one of the boys found in his older brother's bedroom. The magazine had pictures of women who were not fully dressed.

STEP 1: CONSIDER THE CHOICE:
Ask: "What can you do in a situation like this? What choices do you have?" (Use hand motions for Step 1.)
The choice conflict is:
(1) You could just glance at the pictures so that the other boys would not tease you and call you names.
(2) You could choose to tell your friends you don't look at those kind of pictures and risk being teased.

STEP 2: COMPARE IT TO GOD:
Ask, "How do you know which choice is right?" Lead the children to discover that we can know which choice is right by comparing our choices to God.

You may have to ask the children what was wrong with what the boys were doing. They should answer that God wants us to keep our thoughts pure. We can honor God with our thoughts. God is pleased when we cover our bodies properly with clothes. God made clothes for Adam and Eve to wear when they left the garden of Eden. Since then it is God's plan that we cover our bodies properly and keep our minds pure.

Ask a child to find and read Philippians 4:8. (Use hand motions for Step 2.) Lead the children to *admit* that God says we are to think about things that are true, noble, right, pure, lovely, and admirable because that is what God is like. God wants us to think pure thoughts because He is pure.

STEP 3: COMMIT TO GOD'S WAY:
Lead the children to discover that the right thing to do based on God's Word is to avoid looking at those kinds of magazines. (Use hand motions for Step 3.)

Say, "If we *submit* to God, we will choose not to look at magazines that will cause us to think impure thoughts."

Admit:
That God is pure and He does not want us to look at magazines that make us think about things that are impure and wrong.

"Finally, brothers, whatever is true, whatever is noble, whatever is right, whatever is pure, whatever is lovely, whatever is admirable—if anything is excellent or praiseworthy—think about such things" (Philippians 4:8).

Submit:
To God by not looking at magazines that will make us think things that are impure and wrong.

STEP 4: COUNT ON GOD'S LOVING MOTIVATION TO PROTECT AND PROVIDE:

Lead the children to verbally list how God will protect and provide for us if we do not look at the magazines. (Use hand motions for Step 4.) *(God will protect us from guilt and impure thoughts and He will provide us with spiritual rewards and a clean way of thinking.)*

CASE 2

You are home alone and you start flipping through the TV channels. You come across a channel your parents have said you may not watch. You know no one will know if you watch this show. You know the show is not going to be good, yet you are curious about what programs are on this channel.

STEP 1: CONSIDER THE CHOICE:

Ask: "What are your choices? What will happen if you choose to watch shows on this channel?" (Use hand motions for Step 1.)
Guide children to discover the conflict choices below.

(1) You could think looking at the channel for a few minutes will not hurt. Your parents would never know. What is so bad about the channel? You think your parents watch it.

(2) You could choose to watch another program you are allowed to watch, but you would still be curious and wonder about this channel.

NOTE: The children might pick up on a secondary issue in this situation, being disobedient to their parents. If the children want to talk about disobedience, acknowledge the fact, and return to the main issue of purity.

STEP 2: COMPARE IT TO GOD:

Ask, "How do you know which choice is right?" Lead the children to discover that we can know which choice is right by comparing our choices to God.

Ask a child to read Colossians 3:17. Ask, "What does God say?" (Use hand motions for Step 2). The children should be able to answer.

STEP 3: COMMIT TO GOD'S WAY:

Lead the children to tell you which choice would please God in this situation. Ask them to tell you why they think it would please God. Help the children understand that God is pleased when we turn from our selfish ways and *submit* to Him by choosing to do what He says is right. (Use hand motions.)

Thank:
God for protecting us from the bad that comes from impure thoughts and actions.

Admit:
That God is pure and He is not pleased when we watch shows that cause us to have impure thoughts.

"And whatever you do, whether in word or deed, do it all in the name of the Lord Jesus" (Colossians 3:17).

Submit
To God by choosing not to watch shows that are not good for us.

STEP 4: COUNT ON GOD'S LOVING MOTIVATION
TO PROTECT AND PROVIDE:
Ask the children to tell you how God protects and provides for the child who will trust and obey Him. (Use hand motions.) *(God will protect us from guilt and impure thoughts and He will provide us with spiritual rewards and a clean way of thinking.)*

CASE 3

Some of the kids in your group think it is cool to use bad words. At first it was just a word now and then. Lately, it seems like many of the kids are trying to see who can use the worst words the most. You feel uncomfortable, but you want to fit into the group. Should you start saying just a few words when you are with your friends?

STEP 1: CONSIDER THE CHOICE:
Ask, "What are your choices?" (Use hand motions for Step 1.)
Lead the children to state the choice conflicts.
(1) You could think that you would be careful not to use any of these words away from the group. You would just say a few words but not any that directly took Jesus' name in vain. You want to be "cool" when you are with your friends.
(2) You could choose to use wholesome language but you will risk not fitting into the group and you could even lose your friends.

STEP 2: COMPARE IT TO GOD:
Ask, "How do you know which choice is right?" Lead the children to discover that we can know which choice is right by comparing our choices to God.

Ask a child to read Colossians 3:8. Lead the children to understand that because God is pure, His language is always pure. God wants our language to be pure because He is pure. He is the standard for purity by which we should compare ourselves. (Use hand motions for Step 2.)

STEP 3: COMMIT TO GOD'S WAY:
Lead the children to understand that they must *submit* to God by turning away from bad language even if it means losing friends. (Use hand motions for Step 3.)

STEP 4: COUNT ON GOD'S LOVING MOTIVATION
TO PROTECT AND PROVIDE:
Discuss with the children how God protects and provides for a child who commits to turning from her selfish ways and chooses to please Him. *(God will protect the child from being embarrassed when she uses bad language in*

Thank:

God for protecting us from shame and a guilty conscience and for providing us with a clean mind and conscience.

Admit:

That God is pure and He is not pleased when you use bad language.

"But now you must rid yourselves of all such things as these: anger, rage, malice, slander, and filthy language from your lips" (Colossians 3:8).

Submit:

To God by not using bad language.

Thank:

God for protecting you from bad influences and providing you with good friends.

front of people whom she respects. God will protect the child from the bad influence of friends who use bad language. He will provide the child with other friends who do not use bad language.)

10. Use *Truth Works.*
Ask the children to turn to page 14 of *Truth Works*. Give the children time to fill in the blanks. Use "Choosing God's Way" on page 14 for additional practice in applying the Steps of Truth.

    This activity page is almost identical for younger and older children. You may have to do the activity verbally with some younger children.

Provide:
☐ *Truth Works*
☐ *Pencils*

11. Encourage making right choices.
Say: "We will always have to face difficult choices. The good news is that we can trust God to help us make the right choices that please Him. When we choose to obey God, we are protected from the consequences of disobeying Him. We can trust God to always provide for us."

12. Talk about the daily assignments.
Review the daily assignments from the previous week. Ask for a volunteer to say the memory verse for last week. You may want to ask if anyone remembers the memory verses for the last two weeks. Remind them that these verses can help us when we are tempted to make the wrong choice. Preview the daily assignments for the coming week.

Provide:
☐ *Daily assignments*

13. Conclude in prayer.
Praise God for being pure. Confess to God that we do not always choose to do the right things. Ask God to help us obey Him by keeping our minds and bodies pure. Thank Him for protecting us from the harm that comes from disobeying Him. Thank God for loving us enough to provide us with all we need.

RIGHT FROM WRONG®

Love
God Is Love

BIBLE VERSE

"Jesus replied: 'Love the Lord your God with all your heart and with all your soul and with all your mind. This is the first and greatest commandment. And the second is like it: Love your neighbor as yourself'"
(Matthew 22:37-39).

Session Goals

1. CONSIDER THE CHOICE:
   To lead children to consider which choice is right or wrong regarding God's command to love our neighbors as ourselves

2. COMPARE IT TO GOD:
   To lead children to ADMIT that we must compare our attitudes and actions to God's standard of love because God is love

3. COMMIT TO GOD'S WAY:
   To lead children to SUBMIT to a loving God by being obedient to God's command to love our neighbors as ourselves

4. COUNT ON GOD'S LOVING MOTIVATION
   TO PROTECT AND PROVIDE:
   To lead children to thank God for His loving motivation to provide for us and protect us as a result of being obedient to a loving God

Leaders Need to Know

Listen to children talk on a playground. They can say the most unkind, hurtful things to each other. Name calling, teasing, and laughing at the inadequacies of other children are the rules of the playground. Add tattle-telling, bullying, fighting, and ostracizing of certain children to this scene and you will realize that the playground is a vicious place to be.

According to the biblical definition of *love*, love is evident when the happiness, health, and spiritual growth of another person is as important to you as your own happiness, health, and spiritual growth. The Word of God records the command, "Love your neighbor as yourself." This statement does not mean we are to love our neighbors more than ourselves. We are to love God more than we love ourselves, but we are to love our neighbors as we love ourselves.

Through today's session we have the opportunity to teach children God's truth about love. We can lay the foundation about biblical love and how it expresses itself in the care of another person. This foundation of truth will serve the children well as they progress into adolescence.

The material presented in this session is from **Right from Wrong**, *pages 150-156 and pages 208-213. Leaders are encouraged to review this material before presenting this session.*

PRECEPTS

God has spoken clearly concerning how we should treat other people. Consider the following Scriptures.

"You shall love your neighbor as yourself. Love does no harm to a neighbor. Therefore, love is the fulfillment of the law" (Romans 13:9-10).

"You have heard that it was said, 'Love your neighbor and hate your enemy.' But I tell you: Love your enemies and pray for those who persecute you, that you may be sons of your Father in heaven" (Matthew 5:43-45a).

"This is the message you heard from the beginning: We should love one another" (1 John 3:11).

"If anyone has material possessions and sees his brother in need but has no pity on him, how can the love of God be in him?" (1 John 3:17).

"Dear friends, let us love one another, for love comes from God. Everyone who loves has been born of God and knows God" (1 John 4:7).

PRINCIPLE

The principle of love is love for God and love for others. Biblical love requires that we make the happiness, health, and spiritual growth of the person we love as important to us as our own happiness, health, and spiritual growth. In this session we will be specifically teaching children how we should treat others. Children are tempted to make fun of others, fight, be selfish, and call other children names. God wants us to be kind and care for the needs of others. The good Samaritan will be presented as a positive role model for today's children. A discussion about bullies will help the children relate the biblical principle to their everyday world.

PERSON

The principle of love is right because God is love. First John 4:10 defines love. It reads, "This is love: not that we loved God, but that he loved us and sent his Son as an atoning sacrifice for our sins." God initiated love. His love for us is expressed sacrificially. Love is not just something God does, love is who God is. First John 4:8 clearly states, "Whoever does not love does not know God, because God is love."

When we act in hateful, spiteful, or uncaring ways toward other people, we violate the very nature of God.

GOD'S LOVING MOTIVATION TO PROTECT AND PROVIDE

Choosing to obey God and to treat other people in loving ways offers us the following protection and provisions:

1. Protects us from loneliness.
   Provides us with friends.
2. Protects us from bad reputations.
   Provides us with integrity.
3. Protects us from the mistreatment of others.
   Provides us with love from others.
4. Protects us from selfishness.
   Provides us with generous spirits.
5. Protects us from ruined relationships.
   Provides us with good relationships.
6. Protects us from strife.
   Provides us with peace.

Truth Time

INTRODUCTORY ACTIVITIES (10 MINUTES)

The purpose of these activities is to help the children focus on what love is and ways they can show love to others.

"Love Is . . ." Activity
The "Love Is . . ." activity is designed especially for early arrivers. As children arrive, hand them the half sheets on which you have printed *Love Is*. Instruct them to write what they think love is. Tell the children not to put their names on their papers. Let them know that we will use these statements but their names will not be used. Instruct them to place their sheets in a specified box. One leader should quickly read all the "Love Is . . ." statements the children wrote to make sure the thoughts shared in the study group are appropriate.

"Ways I Can Show Love" Activity
Place the gameboard in the middle of the room. Guide children to stand or sit around the gameboard and take turns tossing the beanbag onto one of

Provide:

- [ ] *Poster board*
- [ ] *Markers*
- [ ] *Half sheets of paper*
- [ ] *Pencils*
- [ ] *Beanbag*
- [ ] *A box large enough for half sheet forms*

To Do:

- [ ] *Print* **Love Is** *. . . on the half sheets*
- [ ] *Make a gameboard with poster board*

Ways I Can Show Love	
Home	*School*
Church	*Playground*

Optional idea: draw or find a picture illustrating these four places (home, school, church, and playground) and place them in the appropriate quarter.

Provide:

☐ *Bible*

the four quarters of the poster board. The child tosses the beanbag and tells a way she can show love and be kind in the place where the beanbag landed. Leaders may have to prompt children at first. This game works best with six to eight children. Make a gameboard for each six to eight children.

Study Group Time

(20 MINUTES)

1. Discuss the "Love Is . . ." statements.
   Guide the children to bring their chairs to the study group area and form a semicircle around the study group leader.

   Say: "Thank you for filling out these half sheets describing what you think love is. Let's hear what you think." Read the half sheets but do not identify the writer. Present each thought positively. This can be quite entertaining!

   Say, "Today we are going to learn more about what *love* means."

2. Present the truth about love.
   Open your Bible to Luke 10:25-37. Say, "The Bible story we are going to study today is found in Luke 10:25-37."

   One day a man who was an expert in the Old Testament law asked Jesus a question. The man may have asked the question to trick Jesus, or perhaps he just wanted to see what kind of answer Jesus would give. He asked Jesus, "What must I do to inherit eternal life?" He wanted to know exactly what he had to do to go to heaven.

   Jesus answered his question with a question. Jesus asked him, "What is written in the Law?" In today's words Jesus would have said, "What does the Old Testament say?" Jesus answered him this way because He knew the man was an expert in the Old Testament.

   The man answered Jesus by saying, "Love the Lord your God with all your heart and with all your soul and with all your strength and with all your mind; and, love your neighbor as yourself."

   Jesus was impressed with this answer. His answer was a great one. Jesus said to him: "You have answered correctly. Do this and you will live."

   The man asked Jesus another question, "And who is my neighbor?"

   Jesus answered his question with a story. Jesus said: "A man was going from Jerusalem to Jericho when he fell into the hands of robbers. They stripped him of his clothes, beat him, and went away, leaving him half dead. As a priest walked down the same road, he saw the man and passed on the other side. A Levite also came to the place and saw the hurt man, but he passed on the other side of the road. But a Samaritan came by the hurt man, and he took pity on him. He went to him and bandaged his wounds, pouring on oil and wine. Then he put the man on his own donkey, took him to an inn, and took care of him. The next day he gave two silver coins to the innkeeper. 'Look after him,' he said. 'When I return, I will reimburse you for any extra expense you may have.'"

After Jesus finished the story He asked the expert in the Old Testament, "Which of these three do you think was a neighbor to the man who fell into the hands of robbers?"

The expert in the law replied, "The one who had mercy on him."

Jesus told him, "Go and do likewise."

3. Enrichment idea.
If time permits, review the story by leading the children to act out the story.
Scene 1: Jesus and the Old Testament expert
Scene 2: The traveler, two or three robbers, a priest, a Levite, and the
good Samaritan
Scene 3: The good Samaritan and the innkeeper
Scene 4: Jesus and the Old Testament expert

This Bible story can be easily scripted straight from a modern translation of the Bible. The children can pretend to be the persons in the story, acting out the parts with both words and motions. You can dramatize this story without costumes or props. If you have Bible costumes and can easily assemble some needed props, it will make the experience more exciting. Focus on teaching the truth that God commands us to choose to act in loving ways toward other people.

4. Review the Steps of Truth.
Say: "In this story a priest, a Levite, and a man from Samaria were all three faced with the same choice. Yet they did not all make the same decision." Ask, "How do we decide who was right?"

Ask, "What are the Steps of Truth?" Children who have been present the last three weeks should be able to answer and do the hand motions.

STEP 1: CONSIDER the Choice
STEP 2: COMPARE it to God
STEP 3: COMMIT to God's Way
STEP 4: COUNT on God's Loving Motivation to Protect and Provide

Ask, "When given the choice to act in a loving way toward the hurt man, what did the priest do?" *(He chose to cross the road and pass on the other side. He chose to do nothing.)*

Ask, "When given the choice to act in a loving way toward the hurt man, what did the Levite do?" *(He chose to do the same thing the priest did. He chose to cross the road and go around the hurt man.)*

Ask, "What did the Samaritan do?" *(He chose to help the hurt man. He bandaged the hurt man's cuts and used medicine of oil and wine. He put the man on his donkey and took him to an inn where he could rest. He paid for the man's stay at the inn and left money to care for him.)*

Say: "Pretend the good Samaritan knew the Steps of Truth. Let's go through the steps to review his actions and use the hand motions."

STEP 1: CONSIDER THE CHOICE:

Ask, "What was the Samaritan's choice?" *(He could have chosen to do nothing. Helping the man would cost him time and money. He would even lose some of his friends over it because the hurt man was not liked by the Samaritans.)*

Admit:

God is love and He wants us to love others.

STEP 2: COMPARE IT TO GOD:

Say: "The good Samaritan had to ask himself, 'What is God like and what would God do in this situation?' Can you answer his question?" *(God is love, and He would help the hurt man.)*

STEP 3: COMMIT TO GOD'S WAY:

Say: "The good Samaritan did not just understand what he should do, he acted! He submitted to doing what God wanted him to do. The priest and the Levite were both very religious people who knew the Old Testament Scripture very well. They considered their choices, and they knew that God was a God of love; but the choices they made were not committed to God's way."

Submit:

To God by acting in a loving way toward others.

Ask, "Did the good Samaritan commit to God's way?" *(Yes.)*

Ask, "Was committing to God's way easy for him?" *(Doing the right thing may cost a person his time, money, and effort.)*

Ask, "What did choosing God's way cost the good Samaritan?" *(It cost him time. He had to use some of his own supplies of bandages, oil, and wine to help the man. He had to walk so that the hurt man could ride his donkey. He had to pay money to the innkeeper to care for the hurt man.)*

Reinforce the fact that it is not always easy to do the right thing. At times it may cost us time, work, and money.

STEP 4: COUNT ON GOD'S LOVING MOTIVATION
TO PROTECT AND PROVIDE:

Ask, "How did God protect and provide for the good Samaritan?" *(God protected him from a bad reputation [like the bad reputation the priest and the*

Thank God:

For protecting you from having a bad reputation and feeling guilty about

levite in the story now have]. He protected him from the guilt that comes from seeing someone suffer and not trying to help. God provided him with the honor of having a good reputation and the joy that comes from helping someone in need.)

5. Dismiss the children to their small discussion groups.

Discussion Group Time

(30 MINUTES)

6. Distribute *Truth Works*.
   Lead the children to read the material and fill in the blanks on page 15. You may have to read for younger children. Leaders should discuss the content as they go through the page.

7. Discuss *love*.
   Focus on the definition of *love*. Lead the children to read with you the definition of *love* on the poster.

8. Explore "God's 3-D Love Commands."
   For leaders of older children
   Instruct the older children to turn to page 16 in *Truth Works*. Say: "The Bible has many verses which teach us that God wants us to love Him. Some verses include loving our enemies." Give the children a few minutes to fill in the blanks on this page. Discuss the three commands to love. Some possible answers for ways we show our love are:
   - Showing our love for God.
     We can show love for God when we worship, pray, read the Bible, obey Him, or tell others about Him.
   - Showing our love for others.
     We can show love for others when we help our families, care for a younger child, obey our parents, tell them that we love them, or spend time with others. (Obviously, this list is endless!)
   - Showing our love for enemies.
     We can show love for our enemies when we walk away from a fight, do something kind for someone who has been mean to us, pray for the person who hurt our feelings, refuse to pay them back for what they did, or ask God to help us not hold a grudge.

not helping someone in need. Thank Him for providing you with a good reputation and the joy that comes when you help someone in need.

Provide:
- ☐ *Truth Works*
- ☐ *Pencils*

Provide:
- ☐ *Marker*
- ☐ *Art paper or poster board*

To Do:
- ☐ *On a half sheet of art paper write: LOVE IS caring about the happiness, health, and spiritual growth of another person as much as you care about your own happiness, health and spiritual growth.*
- ☐ *For younger children your poster could read, LOVE IS caring for another person as much as you care about yourself.*

For leaders of younger children
Younger children will have the same basic page. Instead of writing multiple answers, they will draw a circle around the pictures that show examples of love being expressed and draw an *X* on pictures that show unkind acts. Some younger children will not feel they have any enemies. Ask them to think about a child at school who bullies them. They are more familiar with the word *bully* than the word *enemy.* Discuss the pictures and their responses.

Provide:

☐ *Art paper*

☐ *Tape*

☐ *Marker*

To Do:

☐ *Cover the table with art paper.*

☐ *Test the markers to be sure they do not go through the art paper and mark the table surface.*

☐ *On separate pieces of art paper write:* **How does a bully choose to act?** **How does God want a bully to act?** *Tape the paper to the table.*

9. Brainstorm about a bully.
    Say: "It is so much easier to love God and the people who love us than it is to love someone who is mean to us."

    Ask, "Why do you think Jesus said we should love our enemies?" *(God is love. He loves everyone, even those who do not love Him. When we love our enemies, we are following God's example—we are loving someone who does not love us.)*

    Say: "We all know a bully. Each of us has probably been bullied or acted like a bully toward someone. A bully is someone who hurts or picks on someone. A bully may use words or physical actions to hurt the other person. A bully wants his own way. A bully does not care for the happiness or health of other people as much as he cares for himself."

    Say: "There are two questions written on the table. Think of all the possible answers to these two questions and write your answers under that section." Leader, give each child a marker. Monitor the children as they write to make sure they do not use any curse words.

    Review the Steps of Truth with the children. They should be able to quote the four steps and provide the hand motions. If you have new children in your group, take the time to teach the Steps of Truth.

    Read the answers the children wrote under the first question. Ask, "Do you want to be around a person who acts like this?"

    Say: "We have talked a lot about bullies. Our memory verse for this week teaches us that God wants us to love and treat other people the way we want to be loved and treated. The main problem that a bully has is that he is not obeying God. A bully needs to learn that God is love. God expects us to love Him, others, and even our enemies. If you do not want someone to hit you, then you should not hit another person. If you do not want someone to call you names and tease you, then you should not call other people names and tease them."

10. Lead a role-play.
    Lead the children to practice the Steps of Truth through role-playing the following situations. Ask for volunteers to be actors and actresses. Remind the children to use the Steps of Truth to end their scenes.

CASE 1

Kim is very pretty, and she always wears nice clothes. Susan is jealous of Kim. Susan is always saying mean things to hurt Kim's feelings. As Kim walks out of class, Susan pushes her a little and says: "You sure do look cute today. Hope you don't fall and get dirty."

What should Kim do?

STEP 1: CONSIDER THE CHOICE:

Ask, "What choices does Kim have?" (Use hand motions for Step 1).
The choice conflict is:

(1) Kim could push or hit Susan or call her a name.

(2) Kim could do or say nothing to Susan, but Susan would probably keep picking on Kim.

STEP 2: COMPARE IT TO GOD:

Use the hand motions for Step 2 as you ask, "How does Kim know which choice is right?"

Ask two children to read Romans 13:9-10 and Matthew 5:43-45a. Ask, "What is Kim's right choice based on God's definition of *love*?" (Use hand motions for Step 2.)

STEP 3: COMMIT TO GOD'S WAY:

As you use the hand motions say: "Committing to God's way is not always easy. Why do you think it will be hard for Kim to do what God commands?"

STEP 4: COUNT ON GOD'S LOVING MOTIVATION
TO PROTECT AND PROVIDE:

Ask, "How will God protect and provide for Kim?" (Use hand motions for Step 4.) Choosing to obey God and to treat other people in loving ways offers us the following protection and provisions:

1. Protects us from loneliness.
   Provides us with friends.
2. Protects us from bad reputations.
   Provides us with integrity.
3. Protects us from the mistreatment of others.
   Provides us with love from others.
4. Protects us from selfishness.
   Provides us with a generous spirit.
5. Protects us from ruined relationships.
   Provides us with good relationships.
6. Protects us from strife.
   Provides us with peace.

Admit:

That God is love and that He wants us to love even those people who do not act in a loving way toward us.

Submit:

To God by choosing to love even those who do not act in a loving way toward us.

Thank:

God for the way He protects us and provides for us when we love those who do not act in a loving way toward us.

You might ask the children to list other ways God protects and provides if they choose to be loving persons. Their list will be very practical. If a child chooses not to be a violent bully, he may be protected from a black eye or a broken arm. God's provision may be for good health!

CASE 2

Ron wears glasses and has a reputation for being smart and athletic. Frank makes poor grades and has a reputation for being a bully. Both boys are on the same baseball team. During the game Frank calls Ron four-eyes and bookworm in front of the other players. Ron ignores him.

On the way home Frank continues to call Ron names. Frank tries to run over him with a bicycle, but Frank wrecks. The two boys are the only ones there. Ron . . .

11. Choose God's way.
    Lead the children to page 17 in *Truth Works*. Apply the Steps of Truth to the situations the children offer. This workbook page is almost the same for younger and older children. You may have to read more with younger children. Discuss their answers.

12. Reemphasize loving your enemies.
    It is not always easy to act like the good Samaritan. It may cost us to love other people the way God wants us to love. Loving someone who is calling us names or telling lies about us is very hard to do. But God promises to provide good things for us and to protect us from our enemies. We must choose to obey God because God is love.

To Do:

☐ *Pull the perforated assignment sheets from the workbook and have them ready to give to the children.*

13. Talk about the assignments.
    Review the assignments for the previous week. Ask if anyone wants to share an experience from his *Truth Works Journal*.

    Distribute the daily assignments for the coming week. Encourage the children to be faithful to these assignments.

14. Close in prayer.
    Lead the children to thank God for protecting and providing for us when we choose to obey Him by loving others, even those who do not act in a loving way toward us.

Justice
God Is Just

BIBLE VERSE

"He is the Rock, his works are perfect, and all his ways are just.
A faithful God who does no wrong, upright and just is he"
(Deuteronomy 32:4).

Session Goals

1. CONSIDER THE CHOICE:
   To lead children to consider which choice is right or wrong regarding God's command to treat others justly

2. COMPARE IT TO GOD:
   To lead children to admit that we must compare our attitudes and actions to God's standard of justice because God is just

3. COMMIT TO GOD'S WAY:
   To lead children to submit to a just God by being obedient to God's commands to treat others with justice

4. COUNT ON GOD'S LOVING MOTIVATION
   TO PROTECT AND PROVIDE:
   To lead children to thank God for His loving motivation to provide for us and protect us, which comes as a result of being obedient to a just God

Leaders Need to Know

Everyone wants to be treated fairly. The way people appeal to justice when they are mistreated reveals that there is a standard of justice they think everyone ought to know and accept.

PRECEPT

The Bible presents many precepts like:
"Defend the cause of the weak and fatherless; maintain the rights of the poor and oppressed" (Psalm 82:3).

"Give everyone what you owe him: If you owe taxes, pay taxes; if revenue, then revenue; if respect, then respect; if honor, then honor" (Romans 13:7).

"Masters, provide your slaves with what is right and fair, because you know that you also have a Master in heaven" (Colossians 4:1).

The law of Moses contained detailed commands to treat strangers and foreigners fairly. Jesus summed up all of these in one precept, "Do to others as you would have them do to you" (Luke 6:31). These precepts show that God values justice.

PRINCIPLE

Doing to others as you would have them do to you is basic morality reflected in the principle of justice. Justice is foundational to morality. When the foundation stone is removed, morality begins to crumble.

PERSON

God values justice because it reflects the person of God Himself. When we read Deuteronomy 32:4, we learn that justice is not just something God does, but who He is. Because He is just, we can say that justice is right for all people, for all times, and for all places.

GOD'S LOVING MOTIVATION TO PROTECT AND PROVIDE

Choosing God's standards of justice will result in the following protections and provisions:

1. Protects us from revenge.
   Provides for us clear consciences.

2. Protects us from guilt.
   Provides us with peace.

3. Protects us from dishonor.
   Provides us with honor.

Truth Time

ACTIVITY (10 MINUTES)
"BIBLE-VERSE BALLOON BURST"

The purpose of this activity is to help the children discover the meaning of justice and introduce the fact that God is just. Children can burst the balloons and read the Bible verses.

Greet each child as he arrives. Welcome each with a smile and a comment or question that shows you are interested in the child personally.

Explain the balloon game. As you tie a Bible-verse balloon to the back of a child's knee, tell the child that he must burst the balloon to get to the verse. Explain that this must be accomplished without using hands. If you have a large group, let them play the game with partners. Tie one leg of each partner together and tie a balloon to their knees. Explain that they must work together without using their hands to break the balloon and get the Bible verse.

Provide:
☐ *Balloons*
☐ *Bible verse strips*
☐ *Pencils*
☐ *Tape*

To Do:
☐ *Print the following Scripture references on separate pieces of paper. Verses may be used more than once.*
2 Thessalonians 1:6
Deuteronomy 32:4
Psalm 103:6

Zephaniah 3:5
Nehemiah 9:33
Isaiah 45:21
Hosea 14:9
1 John 1:9
Revelation 15:3
Luke 6:31

Provide:
☐ *Art paper*
☐ *Markers*

To Do:
☐ *Print in large letters across the top of a piece of art paper the words* **God is Just**. *Across the bottom, print* **Being just means being fair**.

As each verse is taken from a balloon the child looks up the verse, writes it on the strip of paper, and tapes it to the wall.

Study Group Time

(20 MINUTES)

1. Define *justice*.
Invite the children to join you in a semicircle. Ask for volunteers to read the Scriptures taped on the wall. Say: "These Scriptures show us that it is God's nature to be just. Being just means treating others in a fair way."

2. Prepare for the Bible story.
Ask, "What are some of the choices you make every day?" *(what to eat, what to wear, when to do homework, what to play)*

    Say: "Everyone makes choices every day. Some choices are easy and some are difficult. Some choices are about how we will treat others. We often have to choose to be fair or not fair to someone. Sometimes we make right choices. At other times we make wrong choices. In order to make the right choices we need to compare our choices to God's standard. Today we will explore the truth about justice. God is always just or fair to all people, at all times, in all places. Being just is always the right thing to do."

    Explain to the children that because God is just and fair, He expects us to be just and fair. Every day we must choose between our own selfish ways or God's way.

3. Tell a Bible story.
Open your Bible to Genesis 13. Say, "Abraham chose to follow God by being fair to others." Tell the story of Abraham and Lot.

ABRAHAM WAS JUST

Abraham and his wife, Sarah, lived in Egypt. They had become very rich while living in Egypt. They owned many animals and had a lot of silver and gold. Abraham's nephew Lot lived with them. He had lived with Abraham and Sarah for a long time. He had even lived with them before they came to Egypt. Abraham loved Lot very much.

Then one day God told Abraham and Sarah to move again. Abraham and Sarah took all their animals and all the things they owned and moved to Bethel. Lot also took all the things he owned and moved to Bethel with them. In Bethel there was not enough space for all the flocks and herds of both Abraham and Lot.

They decided they would not be able to live together anymore. They looked at the available land. Part of the land was lush and green and would be better for growing and raising flocks. Cities were near, also. The other land was not so good. Abraham told Lot he could choose whatever land he wanted and Abraham would take what was left. Lot chose the best land for his flocks and herds. Abraham was willing to take the land that was not as good. Abraham was a just man. He was willing to be unselfish and be fair with Lot. God blessed Abraham with much land and many children and grandchildren.

Listen to what God said to Abraham. (Ask an adult leader to read aloud Genesis 13:14-17.)

4. Review the Steps of Truth.

Lead the children to tell you what the four Steps of Truth are and demonstrate the hand motions. Children who have been present for the last four sessions should be able to do this by memory.

5. Abraham and the Steps of Truth.

Say, "Let's use the Steps of Truth to examine how well Abraham did with the choices he faced with his nephew Lot."

STEP 1: CONSIDER THE CHOICE:

Ask, "What choices did Abraham have?" Lead the children to discover the choice conflicts.

(1) Abraham could have told Lot: "I am older. I should get my way. I know that my herdsmen and your herdsmen are not getting along because we need more land for our sheep and cattle. That is not my problem, Lot; it is your problem. I will choose the best land, and you must live where I send you."

(2) Abraham could have chosen to let Lot pick whatever land he wanted. If Lot chose the best land, Abraham would risk getting stuck with the worst land.

STEP 2: COMPARE IT TO GOD:

Ask, "How could Abraham make the right choice?" Lead the children to discover that we can know which choice is right by comparing our choices to God.

Read Revelation 15:3b. Ask, "What does this verse say God is like?" *(God is just. He always does everything right.)*

Lead the children to admit that God is right. Because God is just and fair, we should compare our attitudes and actions to Him and be just. We should do to others as we would like them to do to us.

Admit:

God is just and He wants us to be just and fair with others.

"Just and true are your ways, King of the ages" (Revelation 15:3).

Submit:

To God by being just with others.

Thank:

God for providing peace for us and for protecting us from strife.

Provide:

☐ *Truth Works*
☐ *Pencils*

STEP 3: COMMIT TO GOD'S WAY:

Ask, "How did Abraham choose to *admit* that God is just and commit to obey God and treat Lot justly?" Let the children retell the end of the Bible story.

STEP 4: COUNT ON GOD'S LOVING MOTIVATION TO PROTECT AND PROVIDE:

Ask, "How did God protect and provide for Abraham?" *(God provided Abraham with peace. God protected him from the strife among the herdsmen. God provided Abraham with land as far as he could see. God protected him from poverty. God provided Abraham with many children and grandchildren. God provided him with a good reputation. God protected him from the shame that came Lot's way for choosing to live near people who did not honor God.)*

6. Pray.

Ask God to help the children understand the truth about justice and be willing to submit to God's way.

Discussion Group Time

(30 MINUTES)

7. Distribute *Truth Works* and pencils.

Ask the children to complete page 18. Discuss the questions at the bottom of the page.

8. Lead kid's day in court.

Lead the children to practice applying the Steps of Truth by using the cases on page 19 of *Truth Works*. Guide the children to form a jury. Appoint attorneys to present the case studies and appoint a judge. Ask the judge to read the following instructions to the members of the jury.

The judge says: "I order the jury to use the Steps of Truth to determine if the child in each case was treated in a fair and just manner. You will write your verdict on the sheet provided by this court." Distribute papers to the children.

CASE 1

Sara was selling candy bars for her class during recess. Renee wanted to buy one. Renee had been mean to Sara and had thrown her notebook paper in the mud. Although the candy bars were only twenty-five cents Sara sold Renee a candy bar for forty cents. Renee paid it because she did not realize they only cost twenty-five cents. Sara kept the extra fifteen cents to help pay for the notebook paper Renee had ruined.

Ask the jury, "Was Sara right to charge Renee extra money because Renee had been mean and ruined some of Sara's paper?"

STEP 1: CONSIDER THE CHOICE:
Lead the children to discuss the choice conflicts.
(1) Sara could have chosen to forget what Renee had done and sold her the candy at the same price she was selling it to everyone else.
(2) Sara could choose to get revenge because she felt Renee really deserved it.

STEP 2: COMPARE IT TO GOD:
Lead the children to look on the wall for a verse that would tell them what God is like. Lead the children to discuss why God would want Sara to treat Renee fairly even though Renee had been mean to her earlier.

STEP 3: COMMIT TO GOD'S WAY:
Lead the children to say what Sara should do if she wants to please God and do what is fair.

STEP 4: COUNT ON GOD'S LOVING MOTIVATION TO PROTECT AND PROVIDE:
Discuss with the children how God will protect and provide for Sara if she chooses to say no to her selfish ways and chooses to obey God. If we act in ways that are just and fair God provides and protects for us in the following ways:
1. Protects us from revenge.
    Provides for us clear consciences.
2. Protects us from guilt.
    Provides us with peace.
3. Protects us from dishonor.
    Provides us with honor.

CASE 2

Kyle and Bryce were playing a video game. They were only allowed to play for one hour. Kyle would not give up the controls because he was breaking his previous record. If he shared his video time with Bryce he would not make it to the next level.

STEP 1: CONSIDER THE CHOICE:
Using the hand motions, say: "Kyle has a choice conflict. What are his choices?"
(1) Kyle had been breaking all his previous records. If he shared the video time with Bryce he would not make it to the next level.
(2) If Kyle continued to play and chose not to share the video game time with Bryce he would win five more free games.

STEP 2: COMPARE IT TO GOD:
Ask, "Jury, what would have been the right thing for Kyle to do?" Lead the children to compare Kyle's choices to God.

Ask the children to look on the wall for a verse that would teach them what God is like. Ask them to compare the situation to God's standard of justice.

STEP 3: COMMIT TO GOD'S WAY:
Ask, "If Kyle chooses to submit to God and turn from his selfish ways, what choice would he have to make?" *(give up the game and his chances to win more games)*

STEP 4: COUNT ON GOD'S LOVING MOTIVATION TO PROTECT AND PROVIDE:
Discuss how God will protect and provide for Kyle if he chooses to please God with his attitudes and actions. If we act in ways that are just and fair God provides and protects for us in the following ways:
1. Protects us from revenge.
   Provides for us clear consciences.
2. Protects us from guilt.
   Provides us with peace.
3. Protects us from dishonor.
   Provides us with honor.

9. Apply the truth about justice to the child's own experience.
   Ask the children to turn to page 20. This activity will help children apply the truth about justice to their own lives.

10. Think about what to do when you feel like you want to get even.
    Ask the children to turn to page 21. This activity will provide the children with another opportunity to practice the Steps of Truth. Ask the children to complete their comic strips with their own drawings. If younger children have difficulty, do the activity verbally. Allow the children to share their drawings with each other.

Provide:
☐ *Daily assignments*

11. Discuss the daily assignments.
    Ask the children to share what they learned from the assignments last week. Encourage the children to be faithful to complete their assignments this week.

12. Pray.
    Ask God to help the children choose to submit to Him and treat other people fairly.

RIGHT
FROM
WRONG ®

Mercy
God Is Mercy

BIBLE VERSE

"This is what the Lord Almighty says: 'Administer true justice;
show mercy and compassion to one another'"
(Zechariah 7:9).

Session Goals

1. CONSIDER THE CHOICE:
   To lead children to consider which choice is right or wrong regarding God's commands to show mercy and forgive others

2. COMPARE IT TO GOD:
   To lead children to ADMIT that we must compare our attitudes and actions to God's standard for forgiveness because God is mercy

3. COMMIT TO GOD'S WAY:
   To lead children to SUBMIT to a merciful God by being obedient to God's commands to forgive others

4. COUNT ON GOD'S LOVING MOTIVATION
   TO PROTECT AND PROVIDE:
   To lead children to thank God for His loving desire to provide for us and protect us when we forgive others

Leaders Need to Know

Many people agree that forgiving others is right, but their reasons vary. What is the real reason people should be forgiving? What makes this right? It is right because God is mercy.

PRECEPT

The Hebrew prophet Micah warned his fellow countrymen that their empty religious exercises fooled no one and certainly not God. He told the people that God only required three things of them. The Bible says: "He has shown you, O man, what is good. And what does the Lord require of you? To act justly and to love mercy and to walk humbly with your God" (Micah 6:8). Showing mercy to those we feel deserve it is not too difficult. But what about those who do not deserve our mercy? God is very clear about when we should show mercy and forgive.

"But love your enemies, do good to them, and lend to them without expecting to get anything back. Then your reward will be great, and you will be sons of the Most High, because he is kind to the ungrateful and wicked" (Luke 6:35).

"And when you stand praying, if you hold anything against anyone, forgive him, so that your Father in heaven may forgive you your sins" (Mark 11:25).

"But if you do not forgive men their sins, your Father will not forgive your sins" (Matthew 6:15).

PRINCIPLE

The scriptural precepts mentioned above, which prescribe forgiveness, compassion, and caution in pronouncing and exacting punishment, were given to reflect a principle of mercy.

PERSON

The divine precepts to love mercy and forgive others are right because they reflect God's nature of mercy. Micah presented God as One who "delight[s] to show mercy" (Micah 7:18). David testified that "His [God's] mercy is great" (2 Samuel 24:14). Jesus Christ was the perfect reflection of God's merciful nature. Because God is mercy, we can say that showing mercy by forgiving others is right for all people, for all times, and for all places.

GOD'S LOVING MOTIVATION TO PROTECT AND PROVIDE

Mercy is not only right, but it is also beneficial. Choosing God's standards of mercy protects and provides for us in the following ways:
1. Protects us from want.
    Provides us with blessings.
2. Protects us from retribution.
    Provides us with leniency.
3. Protects us from unforgiveness.
    Provides us with forgiveness.

Truth Time

ACTIVITY (10 MINUTES)
"RIGHT OR WRONG MYSTERY TAG"

The purpose of this game is to introduce the concept of being merciful and choosing to forgive others.

For more detailed information on the principle of mercy, read pages 218 – 224 of the book, **Right from Wrong.**

Provide:
☐ *Construction paper*
☐ *Tape*
☐ *Pen or marker*

To Do:
☐ *Write on each of the pieces of construction paper one of the statements in the following list:*
I lied to a friend.
I forgave a friend who lied to me.
I broke a friend's toy.
I forgave a friend who broke one of my toys.
A friend called me a name.
I forgave a friend who called me a name.
A friend hurt my feelings.

I forgave a friend who hurt my feelings. A friend stole my pen. I forgave a friend who stole my pen.

As the children arrive, welcome them with a smile and a question or statement that shows you care about them personally.

Tape one statement to each child's back without him or her seeing what is on the paper. For each wrong conduct placed on a child's back, place a matching forgiveness statement on another child's back.

Inform each child that you wish to tell her a secret. She is not to tell anyone the secret. Whisper in her ear: "Mercy means you care about others. Mercy means you forgive others who do wrong things even when they don't deserve it."

Tell the children that they are going to play a mystery game to help them practice showing mercy. Say: "I have placed a piece of construction paper on your back, and you must find out what it says by asking questions of the other children. When you find out what it says, you must find your matching partner."

Say: "Your first question will be, 'Did I do something right, or did I do something wrong?' If you did something wrong, you must find out what you did. If you did something right, you forgave someone who did something wrong to you. You must find out what it was the other person did to you."

As the children find their partners explain that they are to become prayer partners. They are to tell each other something about which they are having a hard time forgiving someone. Then they are to pray together, asking God to help them forgive the people who did them wrong.

Study Group Time

(20 MINUTES)

1. Invite the children to join you in a semicircle.
   Talk about what it means to show mercy. Ask, "Who can tell me the secret I whispered to you as you came into the room?" (Allow all to answer at once.) Restate that mercy means to forgive even though a person may not deserve to be forgiven. Say: "When we ask God to forgive us for sin, He forgives us even though we don't deserve to be forgiven. When He does this, He is showing mercy."

   Explain that mercy means caring deeply about others. Say: "When others are hungry, we show mercy by giving them food. When others are sick, we show mercy by visiting them or sending flowers and cards."

2. Present the skit.

Arrange for two adults to present the following skit:

(Lauren and Patrick enter, arguing. Patrick is carrying a paint can and paintbrush.)

Lauren: *I didn't mean to step on your silly ol' snake.*

Patrick: I bet you did. You didn't like Hustler. You probably squashed his head on purpose.

Lauren: *Who me? (She laughs.) What would make you think a thing like that?*

Patrick: You did do it on purpose! You did! You are so mean.

Lauren: *I'm not mean. I just happen not to like snakes and especially snakes crawling around the house.*

Patrick: I'm going to tell Mom.

Lauren: *Go ahead. (She sticks her tongue out and starts for the door.) I'll tell her it was an accident. You know she'll believe me. She won't believe I would do something like that on purpose. (Lauren takes off her pretty new coat, throws it on a chair, and exits.)*

(Patrick drops into a chair and pounds his fist into his hand.)

Patrick: She didn't even say she was sorry. (He looks up toward the ceiling and begins talking to God.) How can I forgive her, God, when she's not even sorry? I know you said I should be merciful, but did you mean to somebody like that? (Patrick looks at his paint can and then at Lauren's coat and smiles. Patrick thinks about getting even with Lauren.)

3. Teach Patrick the Steps of Truth.

Say, "Let's work together to help Patrick make the right choice." (Bring Patrick back into the group and let him sit by the leader.)

Ask: "Children, can you teach Patrick how to use the Steps of Truth and help him make the right choice?" "What is step one?" *(consider the choice)* Request that a volunteer stand and show Patrick the first hand motion. Guide the child in telling Patrick that this means he must consider the choices he has.

STEP 1: CONSIDER THE CHOICE:

What choices does Patrick have?

(1) Patrick could choose to get even with Lauren. He could say he accidently spilled paint on Lauren's new coat. He probably would not get into trouble because Lauren would be afraid to tell on him.

(2) Patrick could choose to forgive Lauren for what she did, but Lauren would probably be mean to Patrick again. Lauren needs to be taught a lesson not to do mean things to Patrick.

Talk about choices. Ask, "If Patrick chooses not to forgive Lauren, how could it help him?" *(He could choose to pay her back, and that would make him feel good for a moment.)*

Ask, "How could that choice hurt him?" *(He could get in trouble himself. He could begin to hate Lauren; hate makes a person miserable. He would not be able to forget the incident and the worry might interrupt his life. He would have no peace with God.)*

Ask, "If Patrick chooses to forgive Lauren, how could it help him?" *(She might be willing to buy him another pet. He would know that he pleased God. He would not be worrying about the consequences and could do other things.)*

STEP 2: COMPARE IT TO GOD:
Request that a volunteer stand and show Patrick the second hand motion of the Steps of Truth. Guide the child in telling Patrick that this means he must compare his attitude and actions to God's standard. Allow various children to read the Scriptures you passed out before the skit: Matthew 6:15, Luke 6:35, and Mark 11:25.

Ask Patrick, "What do you think God's standard or plan is in this matter?" *(to be merciful and forgive her even though she does not say she is sorry)* Say: "God's standard or plan is to forgive because God is mercy. This means everyone should forgive others, no matter what the circumstances." Explain that Patrick should compare his action to God's Word because it reflects God's character and nature.

STEP 3: COMMIT TO GOD'S WAY:
Allow a volunteer to stand and show Patrick the third hand motion of the Steps of Truth. Guide the child in telling Patrick that this means he must *admit* that God is right and *submit* to God's way.

Ask Patrick, "What do you choose to do?"

Patrick says: "I choose God's way. I choose to forgive Lauren."

STEP 4: COUNT ON GOD'S LOVING MOTIVATION TO PROTECT AND PROVIDE:
Say: "That's great, Patrick! You are submitting to God's way. You know, Patrick, when you choose God's way, it places you under the umbrella of God's protection. Everybody show Patrick the fourth hand motion of the Steps of Truth."

Turn to the children and say, "When you show mercy, it protects you from the shame of 'payback' and provides inner rewards." (Ask one of the children to read Luke 6:37-38.)

To Do:

Write the following Bible verses on strips of paper:

"But love your enemies, do good to them, and lend to them without expecting to get anything back. Then your reward will be great, and you will be sons of the Most High, because he is kind to the ungrateful and wicked" (Luke 6:35).

"And when you stand praying, if you hold anything against anyone, forgive him, so that your Father in heaven may forgive you your sins" (Mark 11:25).

"But if you do not forgive men their sins, your Father will not forgive your sins" (Matthew 6:15).

(Lauren enters again and the leader moves to sit with the children.)

Patrick: Lauren, you shouldn't have smashed my snake, but I forgive you anyway.

Lauren: *(She looks surprised.) What?!?*

Patrick: I forgive you.

Lauren: *(She looks at her feet and twists her hands.) I'm sorry, Patrick. I really shouldn't have done it, but I'm really afraid of snakes.*

Patrick: I didn't know you were afraid of snakes. You never told me. I won't buy another one.

Lauren: *I was afraid you'd tease me. (They start walking out.) If you don't have to have a snake, I'll buy you a new pet. What would you like to have?*

Patrick: I don't know . . . maybe an iguana.

Lauren: *Patrick! (She gently pushes him on the shoulder and laughs as they exit.)*

4. Talk about benefits.

Say: "Lauren offered to buy Patrick another pet, but that might not always happen. Sometimes the people you forgive won't say they are sorry after you forgive them. God will bless you for choosing His way, and you will have a clear conscience for doing the right thing."

5. Explain the need to receive forgiveness from God.

Say: "It is right to show mercy to others by forgiving them because God is mercy. To receive God's mercy, we must ask Him to forgive us. Do you know why we need forgiveness?" Lead children to answer that we all have done wrong things.

Say: "Let me tell you a story about the very first man and woman God created. Their names were Adam and Eve."

God made Adam and Eve perfect and gave them a perfect world in which to live. Because He loved them, He gave them the gift of choice. They could choose to love and obey God. One sad day they chose to disobey the one rule God asked them to obey. When they disobeyed God, they sinned. The Bible teaches us that we all have the very same problem Adam and Eve had. We all have chosen our own selfish ways. We have all sinned. Romans 3:23 says, "For all have sinned and fall short of the glory of God." Sin separates us from God and we need His forgiveness.

God loves us. John 3:16 says, "For God so loved the world that he gave his one and only Son, that whosoever believes in him shall not perish but have eternal life." God wants us to live in heaven with Him forever. Because God loves us, we should want to choose His way.

Because God loves us so much, He showed His mercy by sending His Son Jesus into the world to pay for our sins. Jesus died on the cross. The Bible tells us, "This is how God showed his love among us: He sent his one and only Son into the world that we might live through him" (1 John 4:9). We must believe that God sent Jesus to be punished in our place. When Jesus died on the cross, He paid for our sins. Jesus died, but He came back from the dead and has the power to forgive sin.

To receive God's forgiveness we must be willing to turn from our selfish ways and admit that God is right. We need to understand that we have sinned against God and then ask Him to forgive us. If we are truly sorry for our sins and are willing to ask God to forgive us, God will forgive us. The Bible says, "If we confess our sins, he is faithful and just and will forgive us our sins" (1 John 1:9).

When you admit that God is right and submit to Him as your Savior and Lord, He will give you the power to commit to His ways. When you turn your back on your selfish ways, God will forgive you. He will take control of your life if you ask. You can make this decision by praying: "Dear God, thank You for being merciful to me by sending your Son Jesus to die on the cross for my sins. I want Jesus to come into my life to be my Savior and Lord. Please forgive me of my sins and give me eternal life. Make me the kind of person You want me to be. Help me make the choices that please You. Amen."

6. Dismiss the children to their small discussion groups.

Discussion Group Time

(30 MINUTES)

Provide:
- ☐ *Truth Works*
- ☐ *Pencils*

7. Distribute *Truth Works* and pencils.
   Guide the children to work through page 22. Tell the older children to read the page and complete the blanks. Guide them to use the information at the top of the page if they need help. Help the younger children to read the page or ask a volunteer to read it aloud.

8. Discuss the activity "Choosing God's Way."
   Ask the children to turn to page 23 of *Truth Works*. Guide the children to read the situation and complete the blanks. Discuss their answers.
   Discuss the choice each one made. How will the choice help? How will it hurt?

Ask, "What does God say?" Remind them of the Scriptures that were read during the skit. Ask them to add the Scripture verses to the one already in Step 2. Point out that it is God who determines what is right or wrong because of who He is.

Say: "Because God says to 'show mercy,' what is your final choice?" "We must *admit* God is right and do what He does."

Ask, "When you make the right choice, how can you thank God?" Ask them to circle all the answers which they think apply.

9. Show mercy.

   We show mercy when we forgive. Instruct the children to turn to page 24. Let the children try the basketball and dollar bill experiment. They will not be able to hold both ends of the dollar bill if they keep both hands and fingers on the ball. They will have to "let go" in order to receive the dollar bill. Guide the older children to write answers to the two questions in *Truth Works.* Let the younger children tell you their answers.

   Say: "It's the same way with forgiveness. You must 'let go' and forgive others before you can receive forgiveness."

   Let the children work the crossword puzzle. *Forgive* is the answer for each number. They may quickly figure this out, but lead them to find the verses and read them anyway.

   Ask the children to answer the questions following the puzzle. Discuss the fact that God will forgive us according to the way we forgive others.

   Provide:
   ☐ *Dollar bill*
   ☐ *Basketball*

10. Daily assignments.

    Distribute the daily assignments and go over the instructions. Encourage the children to work on these each day.

    Provide:
    ☐ *Daily assignments*

11. Pray.

    Close the session with prayer. Ask God to help the children show mercy to others this week. Pray that the children will want to be merciful because God is mercy.

RIGHT
FROM
WRONG®

Respect
God Is the Highest Authority

BIBLE VERSE

"Show proper respect to everyone:
Love the brotherhood of believers, fear God, honor the king"
(1 Peter 2:17).

Session Goals

1. CONSIDER THE CHOICE:
   To lead children to consider which choice is right or wrong regarding God's commands to respect God and others

2. COMPARE THE CHOICE TO GOD:
   To lead children to ADMIT that we must compare our attitudes and actions to God's standard of respect because God is the highest authority

3. COMMIT TO GOD'S WAY:
   To lead children to SUBMIT to God's way by showing respect to others and those in authority

4. COUNT ON GOD'S LOVING MOTIVATION
   TO PROTECT AND PROVIDE:
   To lead children to thank God for His loving motivation to provide for us and protect us which comes as a result of honoring God and others

Leaders Need to Know

Everyone wants and desires to receive respect. But many of us, including our children, are less likely to give others respect. If treating others with respect is a virtue, it seems to be one that is fastly disappearing from our culture, particularly among our children and youth.

PRECEPT

The first commandment with a promise is found in Exodus 20:12, "Honor your father and your mother, so that you may live long in the land the Lord your God is giving you." God's Word gives us numerous precepts similar to this verse:
1. "The king is enthralled by your beauty; **honor** him, for he is your lord" (Psalm 45:11).
2. "Rise in the presence of the aged, show **respect** for the elderly and revere your God. I am the Lord" (Leviticus 19:32).
3. "Be devoted to one another in brotherly love. **Honor** one another above yourselves" (Romans 12:10).
4. "The elders who direct the affairs of the church well are worthy of double **honor,** especially those whose work is preaching and teaching" (1 Timothy 5:17).

5. "Everyone must **submit** himself to the governing authorities, for there is no authority except that which God has established" (Romans 13:1).

PRINCIPLE

This background information is taken from Josh McDowell's book, **Right from Wrong**, *pages 224-230.*

Respect is the principle behind each of these precepts. The Bible makes it clear that we ought to "Show proper respect to everyone" (1 Peter 2:17). It is easy to look around our society and see the lack of respect.

However, there is another factor to consider. Not only are we to show respect *to* individuals, but we are also to show respect *for* authority. God designed an authority system that we are commanded to respect. The system includes government, parents, teachers, and church leaders. Romans 13 is an excellent chapter to further read on this issue.

Here is a key thought: The person who respects God will also respect those He has allowed to be in positions of authority; therefore, God is honored when we show respect to others in authority.

PERSON

Showing respect to each other reveals the very nature of God. The Bible says that God is spirit (John 4:24) and in Him was life (John 1:4). He is the One who breaths life into us and He is worthy of our respect. We are to treat one another with respect because we are reflections of the God who gives life to everyone.

Additionally, God is God; He is above all. There is no higher power and there is no greater being. "When God made his promise to Abraham, since there was no one greater to swear by, he swore by Himself" (Hebrews 6:13). When we are commanded to respect and obey those in authority over us, we are acknowledging God's authority over all. "For there is no authority except that which God has established. The authorities that exist have been established by God" (Romans 13:1). We can then say that showing respect for other human beings and for those in authority is right for all people, for all times, for all places.

GOD'S LOVING MOTIVATION TO PROTECT AND PROVIDE

Being respectful will
1. Protect us from self-depreciation.
   Provide us with self-esteem.

2. Protect us from harmful relationships.
   Provide us with healthy relationships.
3. Protect us from offense.
   Provide us with attractiveness.
4. Protect us from condemnation.
   Provide us with praise.

Truth Time

ACTIVITY (10 MINUTES)
"KING AM I" GAME

The purpose of this game is to illustrate the respect we should show for someone in authority.

The object of the game is for the children to keep their heads below the level of the king's head at all times. For example, as the king walks, the subjects must walk in a fashion to be under the level of the king's head. If the king bows, the subjects must bow lower, squat, and stay below the king. If the king sits on his throne, the subjects must sit lower than he does. Note: this will be a challenge depending on the body size of the king. As the leader, your assignment is to eliminate any "subjects" who cannot get lower than the king's head. When about half of the children have been eliminated, choose a new king from among them.

Begin the game as the children arrive. Choose the first child to play the part of the king. Place the crown on his head and the fabric material around his shoulders. As time allows, choose different sizes of children to be king.

Provide:
- [ ] *Construction paper*
- [ ] *Colored tissue paper*
- [ ] *Chair*

To Do:
- [ ] *Make a crown out of colored paper.*
- [ ] *Place a chair in the front of the room to represent a king's throne. To further look the part, provide colored tissue paper or fabric material for the child to wear around his shoulders.*

Study Group Time

(20 MINUTES)

1. Discuss *respect*.
   Before the session begins, enlist two leaders to be disrespectful during your presentation. Their assignment is to verbally make comments by interrupting your study time with the children. Position them in the back of the room, behind the children. Instruct the leaders to slowly move forward in front of the children as the process of interrupting begins.

To Do:
- [ ] *Enlist two discussion leaders for the drama scene.*

Ultimately, the leaders will be next to the study group leader and conversing face-to-face. Some example statements may include:

"I do not think she knows what she is talking about."

"Where did she get that information, from a magazine?"

"I think she is trying to be a 'goodie two shoes.' "

"I do not believe a word you are saying."

"Who does she think she is? An expert on respect?"

The object is for the children to see firsthand what being disrespectful is. Cue each other when the final interruption will take place in order to continue the lesson.

Invite the children to join you by sitting in a semicircle. Say: "Today we will be discussing the truth about respect (begin interrupting). We will discover an easy definition for you to understand and how to show respect to those around you. We will also discover ways to show respect in different situations." (By this time, the interrupting leaders should be next to you.)

Turn to the leaders and say: "Do you realize that you are being disrespectful to the children and me? You also are not being a good example in front of these children. Your expressions with your words and actions are not showing respect to someone in authority. Why don't you join the group? We are studying respect, and we can help you understand what respect is." (Ahead of time, encourage the leaders to nod their heads yes and sit among the children.)

2. Define *respect*.

Say: "*Respect* is showing high or special regard for someone, or considering someone deserving of praise and worthy of high regard. *Respect* is an act of giving particular attention to someone. God's Word (hold up your Bible) instructs us to respect everyone."

Provide:

☐ *Bible*

☐ *Poster paper*

☐ *Marker*

☐ *Index cards*

To Do:

☐ *Mark 1 Peter 2:17 in your Bible.*

☐ *Prepare two small signs and two note cards with the following words:*

3. Use your Bible.

Open your Bible and read 1 Peter 2:17 aloud to the children. Say: "We respect others because we first respect God. God is the highest authority. He is worthy of respect. God commands respect because He is God. We treat each other with respect because God made us in His image. You were created with dignity and a purpose. Therefore, every person and those in authority are worthy of respect because we are created in the image of God."

Remind the children that God is above all. There is no higher power than God. God is worthy of respect because God is God, and He is the Highest Authority. God is life and from that part of Him we have life and became a breathing human being. The Bible, God's Word, was sent to us by Him and commands us to respect and obey those in authority. Thus, we admit that God's authority is over us and that He is worthy of respect. Because of this truth, we can then say that showing respect for other people and for those in authority is right for all people, for all times, for all places.

Say: "You must choose to show respect (hold up the card with *show respect*) or disrespect" (hold up the card with the words *show disrespect*).

Say, "We will now dismiss to our discussion groups to further understand and discover the meaning of *respect*."

Discussion Group

(30 MINUTES)

4. Distribute *Truth Works* and pencils to each child.
   Tell the children to read "Respect: God Is the Highest Authority" on page 25 and complete the activity. Discuss the various answers and responses in the activity. The multiple choice answer in the older pupil activity book is the last response, *God is worthy of respect.* Help the children to verbally express the reason we should show respect.

5. Show respect.
   For leaders of older children
   The older children's activity, "God Is Worthy of Respect: Therefore, I Must Show Respect to . . .," is on page 26. Ask them to list people by name under each category. The categories are "My Family," "My Friends," "Authority Figures," and "Others." The "Others" category may include such things as the Bible, property, listening to someone else's opinion, and so on.

   For leaders of younger children
   The younger children's activity, "People I Respect," is on page 26. They will draw one person in each of the four categories in the spaces provided.

6. Discuss being disrespectful.
   Tell the children that everyone has trouble showing respect at one time or another due to circumstances and feelings. Then ask the children to think about this past week when they might have been disrespectful to someone. Complete the activity, "I Was Disrespectful," on page 27. Allow time for volunteers to share some of their situations. Explore how a person feels after being disrespectful. Encourage discussion about individuals with whom they have trouble showing respect and why. Allow time for sharing. Ask the group to respond by giving suggestions on how respect could have been shown.

show respect *and* show disrespect.

"Show proper respect to everyone: Love the brotherhood of believers, fear God, honor the king" (1 Peter 2:17).

Provide:
☐ *Truth Works*
☐ *Pencils*

7. Discuss the problem with respect.

Say: "As you shared your answers from the activity 'I Was Disrespectful,' many of you named the big problem we all have with respect. Showing respect to someone whom we feel is not worthy of our respect is hard, like a teacher who is unfair, a coach who is critical, or a school crossing guard who tries to control everyone."

Read Sue's story and help Sue use the Steps of Truth to choose how to show respect to her stepfather.

SUE'S STORY

Sue and her mother were beginning to settle comfortably in their apartment. It had been three years since Sue's parents had divorced. At first it was very hard, but Sue had accepted the truth about the divorce. Sue had even started to enjoy the extra time her mother had just for her. But her mother started dating. Six months later, her mother married Jim.

Jim had a three-year-old son named Sam. The whole family seemed to shift its focus to Sam. Jim would ask Sue to help Sam dress and clean his room. Sue thought Jim should clean Sam's room himself. She began to resent Jim's demands. Jim also took her mother's attention away from her, and Sue resented that, too.

Because of Sue's resentment toward Jim, she started to talk back to him and disobey him. Sue wants to choose God's way, but she feels so confused right now. What are Sue's choices?

STEP 1: CONSIDER THE CHOICE:
The conflict choice is:
(1) Sue can reason that Jim does not deserve respect. She does not feel he cares for her. He orders her around, but he is not her real father.
(2) Sue could choose to show him respect because he is in a position of authority in her life. However, if she does, he will probably keep taking advantage of her. She wants to obey God, but she feels like she has rights, too.

Ask, "How does Sue decide what is right?"

STEP 2: COMPARE IT TO GOD:
Exodus 20:12 says, "Honor your father and your mother, so that you may live long in the land the Lord your God is giving you."

Children may rationalize that a stepparent is not the real parent; therefore, the child does not have to show respect for a stepparent he does not like. Remind the children that the stepparent is still in a place of authority and should be respected.

STEP 3: COMMIT TO GOD'S WAY:
Lead the children to determine what Sue has to do to follow God's way although it may be hard for her to do.

STEP 4: COUNT ON GOD'S LOVING MOTIVATION TO PROTECT AND PROVIDE:
The good news for Sue is that she can count on the fact that God is totally aware of her situation. He will give her the strength to do the right thing. Lead the children to list ways that God will protect and provide for Sue.
1. God will protect her from guilt.
   God will provide her with peace in her heart.
2. God will protect her from becoming offensive.
   God will provide her with polite attitudes.
3. God will protect her from adding strife to her home.
   God will provide her with a likeable personality.
4. God will protect her from bitterness.
   God will provide her with a loving spirit.

8. Discuss the benefits of showing respect.
   Ask, "What are additional benefits of showing respect?" Encourage the children to look at the two lists in *Truth Works* on page 27. The lists show God's loving provisions and protections for us when we choose His way and show respect to Him and others. Give examples of each and allow the children to share other examples.

9. Practice making a choice.
   Instruct the children to complete the last activity on page 28 of *Truth Works*. The Steps of Truth process will reveal their understanding of the decision making process. Ask for volunteers to share their choices by demonstrating the Steps of Truth.

10. Distribute the daily assignments.
    Distribute the daily activity sheets and briefly go over them. Encourage the children to be faithful to do them.

Provide:
☐ *Daily assignments*

11. Pray.
    Close in prayer asking God to help the children make the right choices this week in showing respect.

Self-Control
God Is In Control

BIBLE VERSE
"Be self-controlled and alert"
(1 Peter 5:8a).

Session Goals

1. CONSIDER THE CHOICE:
   To lead children to consider which choice is right or wrong regarding God's commands to be self-controlled

2. COMPARE THE CHOICE TO GOD:
   To lead children to ADMIT that we must compare our attitudes and actions to God's standard of self-control because God is in control

3. COMMIT TO GOD'S WAY:
   To lead children to SUBMIT to God's way of being in control of one's self

4. COUNT ON GOD'S LOVING MOTIVATION
   TO PROTECT AND PROVIDE:
   To lead children to thank God for His loving motivation to provide for us and protect us that comes as a result of demonstrating self-control

Leaders Need to Know

Self-control within children is needed in today's society, yet many schools, churches, and families struggle to maintain it. Self-control is fastly becoming an outdated truth.

PRECEPT

God gave specific precepts that command self-control.
   "Nor should there be obscenity, foolish talk or coarse joking, which are out of place, but rather thanksgiving" (Ephesians 5:4).
   "But now you must rid yourselves of all such things as these: anger, rage, malice, slander, and filthy language from your lips" (Colossians 3:8).
   "Do not get drunk on wine, which leads to debauchery. Instead, be filled with the Spirit" (Ephesians 5:18).

PRINCIPLE

The principle of self-control is behind each of these precepts. The reason God says to "be self-controlled" (1 Peter 1:13, 5:8) is because God values self-control. God wants us to use the power of the Holy Spirit to control our selfish desires. He does not want our selfish desires to control us.

This background information is taken from Josh McDowell's book, **Right from Wrong**, *pages 230-234.*

PERSON

But ultimately, self-control is a virtue because God is like that Himself. Numbers 14:18 says, "The Lord is slow to anger, abounding in love and forgiving sin and rebellion." God responds slowly and patiently because of His great love for us. Jesus exemplified self-control when He stood before the ridicule and torture of the Roman and Jewish officials and "made no reply" (Mark 15:5).

When we exhibit self-control, we behave like God. We can then say that self-control is right for all people, for all times, and for all places. Self-control is right because God is like that.

GOD'S LOVING MOTIVATION TO PROTECT AND PROVIDE

1. Protects us from excesses.
   Provides us with enjoyment.
2. Protects us from contempt.
   Provides us with respect.
3. Protects us from self-doubt.
   Provides us with self-esteem.

Truth Time

INTRODUCTORY ACTIVITIES (10 MINUTES)

Provide:

☐ *Two buckets of water*
☐ *Two large spoons*
☐ *Two cups*
☐ *String*
☐ *Two bandannas*

To Do:

☐ *Cut the string in pieces 18-24 inches long.*

Suggestion: You pair up the children within their team. If there is an odd number, enlist one of the leaders to play. Tie their legs together. Self-control

The purpose of these games is to allow the children an opportunity to practice self-control. (Choose one or both of the activities.)

"SPOON RELAY"

Play this game with the older children. The object of this game is to fill an empty cup with water. The first team to do so wins. Divide the children into two teams. Form a straight line facing an empty cup. The empty cup should be at least twenty feet away to provide enough challenge for the children. At the starting point, place a bucket of water. Give the first person in each line a large spoon. Instruct the children to fill their spoons with water. Say: "When I say start, you are to walk quickly without spilling your water to the empty cup and put the water inside the cup. Then run back to the front of your team's line and pass the spoon to the next person. The next person will fill his spoon with water and proceed to fill the cup with more water. The winning team is the one who can fill the empty cup with water first." Begin the game.

If time allows, play the game several times by adding a few more restrictions to the players.

"MAKE ME SMILE"

Play this game with the younger children. The object of the game is for one child to make another child laugh without touching him. The two children are to face each other. Decide who will try to make the other laugh first. The child going first may not touch the second child in any way to make him laugh. She may make faces, wave her hands, tell a joke or riddle, or anything else that does not involve touching. When the second child laughs, they switch places—the second child tries to make his partner laugh.

Pair up the children as they enter the room. If there is an odd number, enlist one of the leaders to play. Explain the directions to everyone and then begin the game. If time allows, have a runoff between the children who resist laughing.

Study Group Time

(20 MINUTES)

1. Demonstrate self-control.

   Before the session enlist a leader to help you demonstrate self-control with a food item. Instruct her to sit with the children eating one of your favorite snacks as you begin Truth Time. Your goal as study group leader is to try and resist asking for a snack while you are talking about today's session purpose and goal. Make it obvious to the children that you notice the food. Walk closer to the leader. Smell the air as if you can smell the snack. Make a small comment about that snack being your favorite. You finally give in and ask for a couple of the snack items. At this point begin talking about the definition of self-control and verbalize how hard it is sometimes to have self-control with the smallest of things.

   Invite the children to join you by sitting in a semicircle. Tell the children that today's session is about self-control. Mention that this is the last of the truths discussed in this course. Thank them for their presence each week and for the fun everyone has had together. By this time you should be eating a couple of the snacks. Say: "I thought I could resist eating them, but I just couldn't do it. I did not have the self-control to withhold my urges. Have you ever been this way? Have you ever experienced what I just did?" Allow several children to respond.

2. Share a definition of self-control.

   Ask if any of the leaders can share with the group a good definition of self-control. The leader holding the snack box should stand and take out the clear plastic bag from the snack item box and reply, "I have one." Ask him

definitely will be used as they work together to walk to the cup. Blindfold one person of the paired up team. They could also walk backwards.

Provide:
☐ *Favorite snack item*

To Do:
☐ *Enlist an adult to tempt you with your favorite snack.*

Provide:
☐ *Self-enclosed clear plastic bag*
☐ *Index cards*
☐ *Snack box*

To Do:

☐ *Print the definition of self-control on a card and place the card in the resealable clear plastic bag.* **Self-control is showing restraint over one's own impulses, emotions, or desires.**

Provide:

☐ *Three cards*
☐ *Marker*

To Do:

☐ *Enlist an adult and several children to read Scripture cards.*
☐ *Print the following Scriptures and references on each card: "Do not get drunk on wine . . . instead, be filled with the Spirit" (Ephesians 5:18). "But now you must rid yourselves of all such things as these: anger, rage, malice, slander, and filthy language from your lips" (Colossians 3:8). "Nor should there be obscenity, foolish talk or coarse joking, which are out of place, but rather thanksgiving" (Ephesians 5:4).*

to share his definition. The leader opens the clear plastic bag, takes out the definition card, and reads aloud the definition of self-control.

Thank the leader for reading the definition of self-control. Say: "Some of you have shared already how you sometimes have a problem with self-control. Demonstrating self-control is not always easy when it comes to something you really like. It may be food, money, clothes, video game playing, television watching, or stealing. Self-control is affected by your emotions, your attitude, and your actions. When you have a strong desire for something, your self-control is challenged."

3. Discuss self-control.

Explain how making a choice of self-control, right or wrong, can affect their lifestyles. Say: "Each day you are faced with a variety of situations that require you to make a decision, a choice. That choice can result only in two ways, right or wrong. How do we decide what is the right choice? We must compare it to God and what He says."

Continue to say: "God says that we should allow the power of the Holy Spirit to help us with our self-control instead of our own strength." Ask the person who has the Scripture card with Ephesians 5:18 to stand and read the verse aloud. Say, "People who get drunk with alcohol do not demonstrate self-control." Now ask for Colossians 3:8 to be read aloud. Say, "God asks us to control our emotions and angry words." Ask someone to read Ephesians 5:4. Say, "Again, God cautions us about the words we use."

Ask, "Do you agree that God gave us commands to use self-control?" Allow for acknowledgment. Ask, "Do you believe God is in control of Himself?" Allow for acknowledgment. Say, "Just in case there is a shadow of doubt in someone's mind, let me read Numbers 14:18 to you. It says, 'The Lord is slow to anger, abounding in love and forgiving sin and rebellion.' God uses self-control in showing His anger. He is patient with us."

4. Pray.

Ask God to help each child and adult to rely on the Holy Spirit's power as they demonstrate self-control in their lives every day.

5. Share a Bible story (Luke 4:1-13).

Share the story with the children. Ask the children to share how Jesus was tempted and how He used self-control. Help the children to see that Jesus used a variety of methods to control Himself. He used Scripture and commands. Explain to the children that they, too, can use Scripture when making choices. Jesus is a wonderful example for us. Jesus was tempted just as we are tempted each day, yet He was in control of Himself.

6. Dismiss the study group.

Say, "We will now dismiss to our discussion groups to learn more about self-control and to discover some benefits of showing self-control."

Discussion Group Time

(30 MINUTES)

7. Distribute *Truth Works* and pencils to each child.

Tell the children to read page 29 and complete the activities. Use the question at the bottom of the page as a discussion question. Share with the children that they do not have to wait until a choice has to be made to know whether or not they would choose right.

8. Look at tough times for self-control.

Ask the children to turn to page 30 in *Truth Works*. Use the activity to help children discover situations that require us to practice self-control. The older children will decode words. Younger children will fill in the blanks with words that are provided in the word box.

9. Present the Steps of Truth.

Prior to the session place a basket of pine cones in the center of the discussion table. Say: "We have already said that controlling our anger is a difficult thing to do. Matthew and Ryan had to face this problem together." *Read or role-play the story.*

SUMMER CAMP

Last summer Matthew and Ryan went to a summer camp. They were having a great time until Mike, Ken, and Joe started teasing them and calling them names. As the days progressed, the teasing got worse.

Mike, Ken, and Joe were playing on the hill. When Matthew and Ryan came over the top of the hill, the boys started teasing them again. Mike picked up a pine cone, threw it, and hit Matthew. Mike yelled, "Hey, sissy, bet you can't make a hit!"

There were pine cones all around Matthew and Ryan. Matthew had been a pitcher on the city all-star team, and he knew he could make a hit. It would be easy to hit one of them. He looked at Ryan. Ryan, another city all-star ball player, was angry and ready to fight.

Matthew and Ryan had to make a choice. How could they know what was the right choice to make?

Pick up a pine cone from the basket on the table. Say: "It sure would hurt to be hit by one of these. I can understand why Matthew would like

Provide:
☐ *Bible*

To Do:
☐ *Familiarize yourself with the Bible story in Luke 4:1-13.*

Provide:
☐ *Truth Works*
☐ *Pencils*

The answers for the younger pupil are:
F, F, F, T.
The answers for the older pupil are:
F, F, T, F, T.

Provide:
☐ *Pine cones*
☐ *Basket*

to smash one into Mike."

Lead the children through the Steps of Truth. See how much they can talk through the process and provide the hand motions.

Count on God to:

Protect us from harm.

Provide us with safety.

Protect us from bad reputations.

Provide us with good reputations.

Protect us from hate.

Provide us with self-respect.

STEP 1: CONSIDER THE CHOICE:

The conflict choice is:

(1) Ryan and Matthew could give in to their anger and lose the self-control they have practiced all week. They could choose to pick up pine cones and throw them at the other boys. It sure would feel good to hit at least one of them.

(2) Ryan and Matthew could choose to walk away. They could continue to control their anger and please God with their behavior. If they control their anger, the boys will still tease and bother them. Walking away may look like they really are "sissies."

Ask, "How do Matthew and Ryan decide what is right?"

STEP 2: COMPARE IT TO GOD:

Ask, "Can you recall a Bible verse we heard today that will help Matthew and Ryan?" The children may recall the Bible verse used earlier in this session. If not, lead them to look up Colossians 3:8.

STEP 3: COMMIT TO GOD'S WAY:

Ask two children to role-play the parts of Ryan and Matthew. Allow them to role-play the two choice conflict endings.

STEP 4: COUNT ON GOD'S LOVING MOTIVATION TO PROTECT AND PROVIDE:

Lead the children to verbally list how God will protect and provide for Ryan and Matthew when they choose to follow His way.

10. Use page 31 to apply the Steps of Truth to other situations children face.
    Older children Pair up the older children to go through the Steps of Truth. Each pair chooses a situation and demonstrates to the others how to make a choice that pleases God.
    Younger children Read aloud a situation to the younger children. Lead them to work through the page and the Steps of Truth as a group. Ask for volunteers to demonstrate the Steps of Truth with the hand motions.

11. Pray.
    Close in prayer, asking God to help them make right choices this week in demonstrating self-control. Thank God for the eight weeks you have been together and for what you all have learned. Encourage the children to do their daily assignments even though you will not be meeting again.